SEARCHING FOR WISDOM:
FINDING THE FATHER IN PROVERBS

CONRAD HILARIO

To my sons, Julius and Lorenzo, from whom I draw so much delight.

May you learn from your earthly father's mistakes

and grow wise from heeding your heavenly Father's wisdom,

and above all

that you will trust in the Lord with all your hearts.

ACKNOWLEDGEMENTS

First and foremost, I want to thank my wife, Hilary. You've given me valuable advice and needed encouragement while writing this book. I love you and am grateful to God for putting you in my life.

I am grateful to my mentor Dennis McCallum, for his belief in me and the 19 years he has poured into my walk with God. You've imparted God's wisdom to me as a father imparts wisdom to a son.

Special thanks to James Rochford and John Ross. You guys pushed me to complete this book. Your confidence in my content has spurred me to persevere.

Finally, many thanks to all of the people who helped me edit this book, notably Brad Gabrenya, Liz Hoerle, Pauline Brew, Gwen Herrick and my former college roommate Mike Hahn. I appreciate the time and hard work you all put into this book. I'm indebted to you.

CONTENTS

ACKNOWLEDGEMENTS   6

CONTENTS   7

SEARCHING FOR WISDOM FINDING THE FATHER   9

FATHERS IN THE BIBLE   13

OUR PERFECT HEAVENLY FATHER   25

THE SKILL OF LIVING   35

THE SLUGGARD   47

WORDS AT THEIR WORST   59

WORDS AT THEIR BEST   73

THE DANGERS OF WEALTH   85

STEWARDING YOUR WEALTH   97

FIGHTING FOR FRIENDSHIP   115

GODLY DISCIPLINE   131

HONING YOUR DISCERNMENT   145

SCOOPING FIRE INTO YOUR LAP   157

WOMEN WANT TO BE HER; MEN WANT TO BE WITH HER   173

CONCLUSION   185

SEARCHING FOR WISDOM
FINDING THE FATHER

I must have read the book of Proverbs 10 times before I saw it. Solomon addresses the Proverbs to his *sons*. He opens the book of Proverbs by saying, "Listen, my son, to your father's instruction and do not forsake your mother's teaching" (1:8). Solomon uses the phrase "my son" 19 times. And King Lemuel (who some speculate was Solomon) of Proverbs 31 refers to his son six times.

The book of Proverbs took form in the royal courts as a collection of wisdom designed to instruct Solomon's sons. Solomon had 1,000 wives and fathered an untold number of children. Several lifetimes wouldn't have supplied Solomon enough man-hours to instruct all of his children. So he used a carpet-bomb approach to instructing them, handing them a collection of his wisdom.

But the book of Proverbs expands its application to include anyone who seeks wisdom.[1] The Old Testament frequently uses the Hebrew word "sons" to describe both the men and women of Israel. For example, Moses used "sons of Israel" to refer to the entire nation.[2] So you could easily replace most of Solomon's references to "my son" with "my child." Thus, God supplies men *and* women with wisdom through the Proverbs.

---

[1] The NET Bible note on Proverbs 1:8 states: "It is likely that collections of proverbs grew up in the royal courts and were designed for the training of the youthful prince. But once the collection was included in the canon, the term "son" [*béne*] would be expanded to mean a disciple, for all the people were to learn wisdom when young. It would not be limited to sons alone but would include daughters—as the expression "the children of (*béne*) Israel" (including males and females) clearly shows."

[2] The *Theological Workbook of the Old Testament* states, 'One characteristic formula with the term [*béne*] is "sons of Israel," a phrase that occurs 630 times and is rendered as "children of Israel" by ASV and as "people of Israel" or "Israelites" by RSV and NIV. It is comparable in idiom to "sons of Ammon," i.e. Ammonites."' R. Laird, Harris, Gleason L. Archer Jr., and Bruce K. Waltke, eds. *Theological Wordbook of the Old Testament* (Chicago: Moody Press, 1999), 254.

This small detail contains greater relevance to our culture. A large number of Americans grew up in a broken home. Today, 40-50% of marriages end in divorce. Divorce hit a steep incline, doubling from 1960-2007.[3] In the last decade, the divorce rate has crested and started a gradual descent. But social scientists reason that this is a result of fewer people getting married.[4]

Meanwhile, single parent homes continue to spring up in America. When I talk to students in our fellowship, it's common for them to say, "I don't know my dad" or "My dad is out of the picture." Current estimates tell us one in three children in America lives without his or her biological father.[5] That means nearly 22 million children live in homes without their dads.

Recently, I bumped into an old friend at a coffee shop. We hadn't seen each other in years. As we caught up over a coffee, we discovered that both of us were studying the book of Proverbs. I had been poring through Proverbs to prepare for a new teaching series our fellowship was launching. My friend was preparing for the birth of his first child. So he embarked on a study of Proverbs. But he was reading it through the lens of a father teaching his son wisdom.

You see, my friend grew up without his dad. His dad passed away when he was very young. And his father's absence created a void that left emotional scars in his adult life. He told me, "I want to gain the wisdom my dad was never able to give me and I want to impart that wisdom to my son."

Scripture claims God as its author. The Holy Spirit moved biblical authors to ink God's written word. Thus, Proverbs traces all

---

[3] "Statistical Abstract of the United States: 2011," U.S. Census Bureau, last modified October 2011, https://www.census.gov/library/publications/2010/compendia/statab/130ed.html

[4] Jacqueline Olds and Richard S. Schwartz, *The Lonely American* (Boston: Beacon, 2009), 92.

[5] "Living Arrangements of Children: 2009," United States Census Bureau, last modified June 2011, https://www.census.gov/prod/2011pubs/p70-126.pdf

of its wisdom back to God. He addresses us as a father when he says, "My child, be attentive to my wisdom..." (Proverbs 5:1, NET). Our heavenly Father gave us Proverbs to fill in the gaps left by our earthly fathers.

This book seeks to impart God's wisdom to those who grew up in a broken home and to come alongside people, like my friend, who never received guidance from a father. The first three chapters build upon each other and form a foundation for the rest of the book. The rest of the book covers practical topics such as handling money, choosing our words wisely and building friendships.

This book also aims to pass on wisdom to those who grew up in an intact home. Even the best parents possess character flaws. As we age, we start to see something disturbing. Our parents' flaws begin to appear in our own lives. In some cases, we mimic their example because it seems normal. In others cases, we felt its impact growing up and vowed never to follow it. Yet, we watch ourselves doing the same exact things. Or maybe we've oversteered in the other direction as a reaction to our parent's flaws, but now we've fallen into the opposite yet equal error.

Maybe our parents emphasized certain topics and neglected others. They always talked about diligence but never walked us through how to build a good friendship. This imbalance has thrown our values out of alignment. By contrast, our heavenly Father doesn't suffer from the shortcomings we see in our earthly parents. He speaks to every important aspect of life, placing emphasis on some over others. This sets a pattern for us to prioritize our values. God seeks to correct both our skewed values and our character flaws before we transmit them to younger believers –or worse, to our children.

Before we start looking at our Father's wisdom, we must clear a hurdle in many people's minds. Every spring, the elders of our fellowship escape the city and spend a few days at a beautiful lake house owned by one of our generous members. We use this time for prayer, fellowship and preparation for our annual leaders retreat. One afternoon, we were brainstorming some teaching topics for our retreat and we landed on prayer. Right away, people started claiming passages on prayer they wanted to teach. One of our elders marked out Jesus' parable in Matthew 7, which tells of the son who asks his father for some bread. He felt God was laying a burden on him about the topic of a Father's heart in prayer.

Everyone nodded when he explained his burden. But one of our other elders suggested, "You might want to consider addressing people's negative view of fathers. Many people grew up with abusive or disengaged dads and people tend to project their earthly father's flaws onto God."

Some of our elders shared memories of their fathers. "I have vague memories of throwing the ball with my dad," one shared, "but most of the time his presence was a nuisance." Another described his experience growing up with an alcoholic father, the pain still visible in his voice. "There were times when I wished he was around. But when he was around, I wished he wasn't." Most weren't exactly singing their fathers' praises. Others recounted a mixture of mostly good and some bad experiences.

Before we hear from our heavenly Father, we need to see him without our earthly father's flaws. In the next chapter, we will scour the Bible to find examples of fathers.

FATHERS IN THE BIBLE

When I took my first stab at reading the Old Testament, it startled me how honestly God depicted biblical characters. The Bible doesn't flatten biblical characters into moral object lessons. Like unedited movie footage, God gives us the raw, uncut version of biblical characters. Scripture depicts men and women just as complicated and sinful as you or me.

Therefore, it shouldn't surprise us to find imperfect examples of fathers in the Bible. They struggled with the same problems fathers face today. Let's take a tour through the Old Testament and look at a few examples of fathers.

Lot: The Compromised Father

When God called Abraham to leave his home in Ur, he brought along his nephew Lot. But as they were traveling, Abraham's and Lot's herdsmen began quarrelling with each other. To alleviate tension between their herdsmen, Abraham and Lot chose to part ways. Abraham said to Lot, "There's plenty of land for us to settle. I'll go left. You go right." Lot looked up and saw that the plain of the Jordan "was well watered, like the garden of the Lord" (Genesis 13:10). So Lot chose to settle in Sodom, a city located on the Jordan plain. And Abraham settled further West in the land of Canaan.

Sodom was a city brimming with opportunities. Jesus gives us a thumbnail of life in Sodom, "People were eating and drinking, buying and selling, planting and building" (Luke 17:28). Industry was booming in Sodom. People were engaged in commerce. Sodom was growing, with new buildings popping up all over the city. And the people enjoyed fine dining and a vibrant nightlife.

With hard work and a will to succeed, you could earn a fortune in this city. Lot had already prospered under the Lord's hand, possessing large flocks, herds and employees. Sodom merely represented the next step toward Lot's quest to become wealthy. But it was also the first step toward compromise.

Materialism ran rampant in this city. Sodom turned a blind eye to its impoverished residents. The prophet Ezekiel casts this railing judgment upon the city, "Now this was the sin of your sister Sodom: She and her daughters were arrogant, overfed and unconcerned; they did not help the poor and needy" (Ezekiel 16:49).

In many ways, Lot resembles many modern American Christians. They claim to live for Christ. But when you look at their lives, it seems like the world shapes their values more than God does. Just like Lot, they make major life decisions based solely on money and career advancement. Often, they make decisions like this at the expense of their family, friends and spiritual community. They uproot themselves and their families because of an opportunity they "just can't pass up."

Fast-forward twenty-five years. Lot has put down roots in Sodom. He's grown comfortable living in this prosperous city. Lot has probably increased his net worth since living there. There's even evidence Lot occupied a prominent political position. When the two angels (disguised as men) entered the city, they found Lot "sitting in the gateway of the city" (Genesis 19:1). City officials would meet at the city gate. By all accounts, Lot gained wealth, influence and power while living in Sodom. But little did he know God was planning to destroy the city he'd grown to love.

When Lot sees the two angels, he invites them into his house. That evening, a large crowd of men (both young and old) surround Lot's house. Intending to force themselves upon these men, they cry out, "Bring them out!" Lot slips out the front door and quickly closes it behind him. Holding his arms out as if to block them from coming through the door, he says, "Don't harm these men, they're under my roof of protection." Ancient near eastern custom bound one to protect guests staying in their home.

"I have two daughters," Lot says, "They've never been with a man. Take them." Lot was drowning in the values of his culture. He was more committed to upholding the customs of his culture than he was the well-being of his daughters. Some of the men fire back, "You move to our city and now you dare judge us?" They were confronting Lot for his hypocrisy.

The two angels pull Lot back into the house and force the door closed. Then the two angels strike the men of the city blind. However, this didn't deter them. Moses offers this detail, "The men outside wore themselves out trying to find the door" (Genesis 19:11, NET). Can you imagine the men of this city groping around, trying to find their way into Lot's house?

The two angels tell Lot of God's coming judgment and urge him to get his family out of the city. Lot flees to his future sons-in-law's house to warn them about God's judgment. Breathless, he cries, "Get out of the city, now! The Lord is going to destroy it." But his sons-in-law just laugh at him. It's not clear why. Perhaps Lot didn't seem too eager to leave the city himself. Maybe they thought, "Here he goes, talking about that God stuff again." Whatever the reason, Lot carried no moral authority with his family. Like so many Christian fathers, Lot probably talked more about the things of God than he was willing to put into action.

The two angels urge Lot and his family to escape the city. But...Lot hesitates. He has a hard time leaving the city he has grown to love. Lot might have expressed moral outrage over the city's depravity, but he doesn't seem to have a critique of its values. The allure of materialism had seduced Lot. And he enjoyed the recognition that came from occupying an important political position. The two men practically drag Lot and his family outside of the city.

Once they're safely outside the city, the two men urge Lot, "Run! Don't look back or stop. Otherwise, you'll be destroyed too." Lot pleads with them to spare a small town in the Jordan plain. He was clinging to his former life. The two men reluctantly grant Lot's request.

Sulfur and fire rain down upon Sodom and Gomorrah while Lot and his family flee. But Lot's wife looks back and freezes dead in her tracks. She turns into a pillar of salt. The Hebrew word for "look" means "to gaze intently or longingly." Lot's compromise not only afflicted his spiritual life, it had spread to his family.

Lot represents an example of compromise. He talked a lot about the things of God, but never really lived them out. And his compromise took a toll on his kids' spiritual lives (Genesis 19:30-38). When kids see their parents' hypocrisy, it makes Christianity unappealing. There's nothing worse than hearing someone bluster about their convictions, only to see flaccid follow-through. Some kids react by rebelling against Christianity. Worse, some adopt their parents' compromised faith.

Eli: The Permissive Father

Eli served at the Tent of Meeting as God's high priest. He had two sons named Hophni and Phineas. They followed in their father's footsteps, serving as priests. Yet, unlike their father, Hophni and Phineas "had no regard for the Lord" (1 Samuel 2:12). They took portions of meat reserved for those offering the sacrifice.

According to the Law of Moses, the priest was to offer the fat portions of the animal (the tail, kidneys and a portion of the liver). He could reserve the breast and thigh meat for himself. But the Law directed him to give the rest of the animal to the person offering the sacrifice. Eli's sons were taking their portion *and* the rest of the animal. Even worse, Hophni and Phineas were demanding portions of meat before sacrificing the fat portions.

At one point, the people beg Hophni and Phineas, "At least offer the sacrifice first and then take whatever you want." But Hophni and Phineas leave them with no other option, "Give it to us now, or else we'll just take it from you." According to Samuel, their sins were "very great in the Lord's sight, for they were treating the Lord's offering with contempt" (1 Samuel 2:17).

But things go from bad to worse. Hophni and Phineas start sleeping with the women stationed at the entrance of the Tent of Meeting. Finally, the text tells us that Eli confronts his sons "in his old age" (1 Samuel 2:22). Biblical scholar Kenneth Chafin elaborates,

> The phrase *"Eli was very old"* suggests a kind of helplessness to control his sons at this point in their lives. There may have been a time when his words might have changed things, but that

time is long past. His speech is but a reminder of the depths to which his sons had gone in their abuse of position.[1]

Yet, Hophni and Phineas refuse to listen to their father despite his pleas. Did Eli seriously expect them to listen, after years of tolerating their behavior? Eli's window of opportunity closed years ago.

Eli embodies the picture of a permissive father. He was only willing to say something when it was painfully obvious that his sons were abusing their office. Samuel tells us Eli "heard about everything his sons were doing" three times (1 Samuel 2:22). Did he finally say something because people were urging him to intervene? Some permissive parents will eventually open their mouths, but often when it's too late. In many cases, they could've disrupted a trend before it hardened into a pattern of behavior.

Why was Eli reluctant to discipline his sons? Samuel gives us the answer. In 1 Samuel 2:29, God asked Eli this incriminating question, "Why do you give your sons more honor than you give me?" Eli idolized his sons. That's what drove his permissiveness. And the Lord added, "For you and they have become fat from the best offerings of my people Israel!" (1 Samuel 2:29, NLT). Apparently, Eli wasn't complaining about the choice cuts of meat his sons were bringing home.

Some of us grew up with parents like Eli. Their softness has created problems for us in our adult lives. Like Eli's sons, we're accustomed to getting what we want. We see ourselves as the axis on which the world turns. As a result, we use people around us to satisfy our selfish desires.

David: The Disengaged Dad

David ruled during the golden age of Israel. He showed brilliance as an administrator, raising the nation of Israel to power and glory in a short time. He exhibited military genius, leading Israel's army

---

[1] Kenneth L. Chafin and Lloyd J. Ogilvie, *The Preacher's Commentary Series* (Nashville, TN: Thomas Nelson Inc, 1989), 37.

to countless victories. Like a bottomless fountain, he produced an endless stream of music and poetry. Despite all of these accomplishments, he wasn't able to deliver as a father. David led an entire nation, but couldn't lead his own family.

Trouble started when David's eldest son (Amnon) fell in love with his half-sister (Tamar). Amnon's sexual appetite held him prisoner, just as it did his father. Sick with desire for Tamar, Amnon tried to seduce her. But when she resisted his advances, he forced himself upon her.

When David heard about what happened, he was furious with Amnon. But the text remains silent about David saying anything to him. David refused to do anything about Amnon's sin. Maybe David felt like he was standing on shaky moral ground because of his own incident with Bathsheba. The Greek translation of the Old Testament gives us a clue. It adds that David "would not punish his son Amnon, because he loved him, for he was his firstborn."[2]

Meanwhile, Tamar's brother (Absalom) was boiling with anger toward Amnon. For two long years, Absalom waited for the right moment to get revenge for his sister's rape.

During the annual sheep-shearing festival, Absalom invites his father and his father's servants to join him. But David replies, "We shouldn't all go. It would be too much of a burden on you." David was probably making excuses. Maybe he faced an urgent matter in the kingdom. Like most disengaged dads, David always gave a reason for why he had to miss an event.

Absalom sees his opportunity. He relays this message to his father, "If you can't come, send my brother Amnon." This arouses David's suspicion. David asks Absalom, "Why do you want Amnon to go?" David senses lingering tension between his sons over Tamar. Apparently, he didn't do anything about it. David

---

[2] 2 Samuel 13:21, LXX.

used shrewd diplomacy when dealing with kings, but he couldn't even mediate conflict within his own family.[3]

But Absalom presses David to send Amnon and David finally gives in to his request. Did David concede because he felt guilty about his lack of involvement? Disengagement typically gives way to permissiveness.

Right before the festival, Absalom hatched a plan to murder his brother. "When Amnon has had too much to drink, strike him down," Absalom instructed his servants. At Absalom's signal, they carried out the plan.

How could David be so naive? David showed brilliance in leadership throughout his career. He was aware of "everything that happens in the land [of Israel]" (2 Samuel 14:20). Perhaps David couldn't see what was happening because he was too close to the situation.

In many ways, David resembles countless fathers today: highly capable at work and yet completely inept at home. I've met men whom most consider experts in their field. They possess the natural ability to lead people, managing dozens or even hundreds of employees. But when they come home at night, they look confused and tired. They give the best hours of their day to work, leaving little else for their family. Disengagement not only destroys families, it impacts a man's ability to serve God.

After killing Amnon, Absalom flees the capital and goes into hiding. Three years pass and eventually David allows Absalom to return. But there's a catch. Absalom can live in the capital, but he cannot see the king. Two more years pass before David permits Absalom to enter his court. During this time, Absalom develops resentment toward David and plans to usurp the throne. Eventually, Absalom wins the hearts of the people and deposes

---

[3] We find an example of David's diplomacy in 1 Samuel 30:26-31, where he gave the elders of Judah the plunder from his battle with the Amalekites. David was probably trying to curry favor with them before occupying the throne.

David. Had David sought to reconcile sooner, he might've avoided this overthrow.

It would take nearly four years before David sat back on the throne, yet it came at a great cost. Absalom arrayed his troops against David's men. But they were no match for David's battle-hardened army. David's troops easily routed Absalom's army. During their retreat, one of David's men killed Absalom.

When David hears the news of Absalom's death, grief overwhelms him. He wanders through the streets, stumbling at the city gate, where he falls to his knees and cries out, "O my son Absalom! O Absalom, my son, my son!" (2 Samuel 19:4) David wasn't a stranger to death and violence. He even experienced the grief of losing a child. But we never see David mourn like this. His mourning was probably a mixture grief and guilt. Surely, he saw his responsibility in Absalom's revolt. Had he done something about Tamar, had he reconciled with Absalom sooner, maybe Absalom would still be alive. At that moment, maybe David discovered how much his family meant to him. But it was too late. Kenneth Chafin summarizes this chapter in David's life, "It closes on one of the saddest notes in David's life, when as a broken-hearted father he sobs out his grief at the death of his son whom he had really lost years before."[4]

This wouldn't be the last time David experienced betrayal from one of his sons. David's son Adonijah tried to depose him while David laid on his deathbed. Adonijah should've succeeded David on the throne, but instead God chose Solomon. If Adonijah wanted the throne, he had to take it by force. Again, we can trace a line of guilt right back to David for Adonijah's rebellion. The author of 1 Kings adds this comment about David's relationship with Adonijah, 'His father had never interfered with him by asking, "Why do you behave as you do?"' (1 Kings 1:6). Adonijah grew accustomed to getting what he wanted. The throne was no exception.

---

[4] Chafin and Ogilvie, *Preacher's Commentary*, 319.

Throughout his reign, David showed that he was a very capable person. God endowed him with immense creativity and inspired David to compose nearly half the Psalms. He managed to solidify most of the kingdom during his reign, personally leading Israel's army in battle. He led Israel into its golden age, showing his ability to govern. But his personal life didn't match his public life. David was absent from his kids' lives. He was more absorbed with his duty as a king than as a father.

Some of us grew up with a father like David. He spent countless hours at work instead of spending time with us. Our father always seemed disconnected from us. Many of us learned that storming out of the room or starting a fight were the best ways to get his attention. Or we could grab his attention if we performed well in school or sports.

In adulthood, we find ourselves placing heavy love demands upon our family and friends. When we feel like people aren't loving us the way they should, we simmer with anger. Over time, those closest to us buckle under our crushing expectations. They either slowly distance themselves from us or learn to avoid our bad moods like potholes in the road.

Absence of Good Fathers in the Bible

Scripture presents numerous examples of godly men. Job brought sacrifices to the Lord on behalf of his children. Abraham showed loyalty to God when he planned to carry out the sacrifice of his son Isaac. Joshua publicly pledged his and his family's service to the Lord. Yet, Scripture never explicitly extols someone for being a good father. Like trying to search for a lost sock in the laundry, it's difficult to find one example of a good father in the Bible.

Scripture provides far more examples of godly mothers. The Bible applauds Samuel's mother Hannah, for dedicating him to the Lord's service as a young boy (1 Samuel 1:21-28). Throughout Samuel's life, Hannah continued to express her love for her son. Several times a year, she made the journey to see him in Jerusalem and bring him expensive clothing (1 Samuel 2:18-19).

We see more examples of extraordinary mothers when we turn to the pages of the New Testament. Timothy grew up with women who possessed deep faith in God. Luke places the spotlight on Timothy's mother (Eunice) for her faith (Acts 16:1). And Paul describes Timothy's grandmother (Lois) as possessing "sincere faith" (2 Timothy 1:5). Timothy's earliest memories were of his mother and grandmother instructing, persuading and encouraging his faith in God (2 Timothy 3:14-15).

Maybe the best example comes from Jesus' own upbringing. The New Testament introduces Mary as a woman with deep faith in God. Mary accepted God's call to bear his son even though it would probably cause Joseph to end their engagement. She said 'yes' to God even though it would likely heap public shame upon her parents. Unlike today, ancient Jewish culture condemned premarital sex. Her parents would probably suffer financial loss if she agreed to bear the son of God. In the ancient world, a bride's parents would give the groom and his family a security deposit guaranteeing the marriage. Can you imagine Mary telling her parents about this? "Mom, Dad, let me tell you about this great thing that happened after school today." After Jesus' birth, she withstood years of people whispering about the real identity of his father.

To make matters worse, Mary probably raised Jesus as a single mom. Jesus' father (Joseph) appears in accounts of Jesus' early life, but then he vanishes from the narrative. Most commentators presume Joseph died when Jesus was a teenager.[5] His absence left Mary to raise Jesus along with his six siblings (Matthew 13:55-56).

And yet, Mary squeezed time out of her busy schedule to teach Jesus the Scriptures. Luke summarizes his early life in Luke 2:52, "Jesus kept increasing in wisdom and stature and in favor with God and men" (NASB). Even though Mary bore the full weight of supporting a large family, she carved out time to influence Jesus spiritually.

---

[5] Scripture doesn't mention Joseph after the episode where he and Mary found Jesus in the Temple.

Some of us can relate to the biblical examples we've examined. We grew up either with a single mom or a disengaged dad. As a result, we resonate with some of the deficits described above. God wants us to see that he can sort out the mess this has created in our lives. He can nurture us out of these destructive patterns and help us overcome our deficits. He wants to assume the role of our perfect heavenly Father. Although our earthly fathers made many mistakes, our heavenly Father loves us perfectly.

For Further Discussion:

1. Why do men in our culture seem emotionally and relationally disengaged?
2. How has your earthly father impacted your view of God either positively or negatively?

OUR PERFECT HEAVENLY FATHER

When Jesus burst onto the scene, no one would've guessed he would flip the Jewish religious system on its head. Today, we wouldn't bat an eye if we heard people refer to God as their father. But in ancient Jewish culture, if you referred to God as your "Father," every jaw in the room would drop. Up to this point, no one addressed God as his or her father. But that was classic Jesus. He spoke to God as a father, expressing the kind of intimacy they shared. As believers in Christ, God has given us this same privilege. We can share the same intimacy Jesus shared with the Father. That's what John means when he says, "To all who received him, to those who believed in his name, he gave the right to become children of God" (John 1:12).

Our status changes the instant we forge a relationship with God through Christ. He adopts us as his sons and daughters. In the ancient world, if someone adopted you, that person didn't look at you as a second-rate son or daughter. You possessed the full rights of a natural heir. Paul writes to the Ephesian believers, "For [God] chose us in [Christ] before the creation of the world to be holy and blameless in his sight. In love he predestined us to be adopted as his sons in Jesus Christ" (Ephesians 1:4-5). God chose to adopt us even before laying the foundation of the earth. God not only guarantees us eternal life as part of our inheritance, he also promises to crown us as kings and queens. Paul spells this out in Romans 8:15-17:

> For you did not receive a spirit that makes you a slave again to fear, but you received the Spirit of sonship. And by him we cry, 'Abba, Father.' The Spirit himself testifies with our spirit that we are God's children. Now if we are children, then we are heirs— heirs of God and co-heirs with Christ.

Although it's easy to grasp the concept of God as *a* father, it's often hard to view God as *our* Father. For many of us, the image of a father carries a lot of baggage. We tend to take bad experiences we've had with our earthly fathers and project them onto God. At other times, we superimpose our earthly fathers' weaknesses onto God.

God wants to overwrite our negative view of fathers as we get acquainted with him. But this won't happen immediately. You can't build trust overnight. However, we can start this process by looking at some of the differences between our earthly fathers and our heavenly Father.

Involved

Many of us grew up with disengaged dads. We can bring to mind images of Dad sitting on the couch, zoned out in front of the screen after work. A long day at work left him too exhausted to engage us about our day. Growing up, he hardly ever talked to us about our fears or worries.

By comparison, God immerses himself in our lives. He indwells us with his Spirit the moment we receive Christ, which guarantees his presence in our lives. His eye remains upon us throughout the day, from the moment we rise to the moment we lay our head down to sleep. Moreover, his omniscience allows him to see our strengths, our weaknesses, our drives and our potential. After all, he handcrafted us. David showed his awareness of this when he wrote, "You created my inmost being; you knit me together in my mother's womb...All the days ordained for me were written in your book before one of them came to be" (Psalms 139:13, 16).

Scripture's view stands in sharp relief to many modern concepts of God. Most people in our culture believe God exists, but the god they imagine resembles a deistic god, who wound up the universe and walked away. We can't say this about our heavenly Father. He wants to hear about what's rattling around in our minds. He even wants to hear about the most mundane aspects of our lives. Take a moment to list all the things that worry you throughout the day. These worries quietly run in the background, producing low-grade stress and anxiety. Yet, the thought never pops into our heads, "I should talk to God about this." We don't regard them as important enough to bring to him. After all, why would God want to listen to me talk about my phone bill or about finding my wallet? Scripture challenges us to "not be anxious about anything" (Philippians 4:6). God longs to hear about what has been bothering us, no matter how mundane it may seem.

You would think this kind of open access to God would cause us to turn to God whenever we feel anxious, but that's often the last place we look to find relief from our stress and worry. Why do we fail to take advantage of our exclusive access to God? As it turns out, our pride often blocks us. That's why Peter encourages us to "humble [ourselves], therefore, under God's mighty hand, that he may lift [us] up in due time. Cast all your anxiety on him because he cares for you (1 Peter 5:6-7)." It requires humility to unload our anxieties onto God because we're giving him access to our lives.

Shows Unconditional Love

God chose to adopt us before he set the footing for the foundation of the world. He planned to send his son Jesus before we were even born. God was aware of all the moral wrongdoings we would commit during our lifetimes and paid for them two thousand years ago on a cross. Thus, when we experience moral failure, God doesn't withdraw his love from us.

We never have to cower when entering God's presence. As John tells us, "There is no fear in love. But perfect love drives out fear" (1 John 4:18). Even when we fall into sin, we can confidently approach God. That's why the author of Hebrews urges us, "Let us draw near to God with a sincere heart in full assurance of faith, having our hearts sprinkled to cleanse us from a guilty conscience and having our bodies washed with pure water" (10:22). God never looks upon us with disappointment or anger. He doesn't hold grudges against us. He has completely washed away our sins through Christ. Now we can boldly walk into his presence without shame, guilt, or fear.

Further, God comes from a position of complete security. He doesn't look to us to meet his needs. Even the best parents place certain expectations on their children. All parents want the best for their kids, but sometimes this desire morphs into parents trying to live out their unfulfilled dreams through their children. You see this when parents coach their kids from the stands at a sporting event, or run onto the field and yell at a referee about a bad call. Some parents turn to their children for their relational needs, bombarding them with phone calls and suffocating them with love demands. By contrast, our heavenly Father doesn't demand love from us. Instead, he looks to himself in order to satisfy his relational needs (John 17:24). This allows him to lavish love upon us without expectation.

Eager to Provide

Some of us grew up in homes where Dad wasn't around to provide for our families. Or, like a barnacle attached to a whale, he lived with us but didn't contribute. By contrast, God promises to meet all of our needs. Our spiritual adoption guarantees it. God the Father possesses endless resources. Couple this with his constant awareness of our needs, and you can count on him to take care of us.

Our Father gave proof of his total commitment to us when he sent his one and only Son to die for us. God gave up his most prized possession to redeem us from the sentence of death. Paul asks, "He who did not spare his own Son, but gave him up for us all — how will he not also, along with him, graciously give us all things?" (Romans 8:32). Paul uses a type of argument that we no longer use today. He's taking a lesser thing and comparing it to something greater. "If this is true, then how much *more* must that be true?" Following Paul's argument, if God didn't spare his beloved son to rescue us, how much more will he provide for our basic needs?

Once a week, I wake up with my kids so my wife can sleep in. My two-year-old son's internal alarm clock goes off at 6 a.m., sometimes 5:30. I'm not what you would call a morning person. So when my son calls for me, I pick him up and lurch down the stairs with my eyes half open. When we get downstairs, I collapse on the couch to get more sleep. But he starts pawing at me like a little bear cub begging for food. So I bid my body to climb off the couch and prepare breakfast for my son. Now if my imperfect love for my son drives me to take care of his needs, how much more will our heavenly Father's perfect love meet our needs? He doesn't suffer from human frailties such as tiredness or selfishness.

Some of us carry a crushing weight of anxiety. Our minds start to spin as we figure out how we're going to pay our bills. We stress about getting a career that will provide for a family. Thoughts of the future overwhelm us. Like a mortar and pestle, worry grinds us down as we look to meet our own needs.

God tells us to stop worrying. In fact, he equates worry with a lack of faith. God assumed the responsibility of providing for our needs the moment he adopted us. We don't have to worry about how we're going to pay our rent or if we'll have enough money left in our pockets to eat. God promises to cover the red ink if we're doing our part by working hard and handling our money carefully. There have been times in my life when the end of the month was quickly approaching and I didn't have enough money to pay my bills. In each case, God provided for my family and me. At times, he did it when the clock was about to expire, but he has never failed to provide.

Emotionally Engaged

For others of us, Dad was highly involved in our lives. He did activities with us, like playing sports or fishing. He worked hard to provide for our family. At the same time, it was difficult for him to connect with us emotionally. He seemed uncomfortable talking about anything beyond surface or practical matters. He would ask us about our day at school or talk about some interesting fact he found on the Internet. But if we seemed depressed, he would try to cheer us up by taking us shopping. Or he would utter a platitude or make light of the situation and quickly change the subject.

Our perfect heavenly Father doesn't suffer from fear of intimacy. If we want to catch a glimpse of God's eagerness to connect with us, we should examine Jesus' life. Jesus embodied God's ultimate revelation. God revealed more about himself through Jesus than through all of the Old Testament prophets combined (John 14:8-9).

Throughout the Gospels, Jesus expresses a variety of emotions. He showed compassion when he saw the lost multitudes (Mark 6:34; Matthew 20:34). He was unable to choke back sobs when he approached Lazarus' tomb (John 11:35). He vented his moral outrage toward the moneychangers, flipping over their tables and driving them out of the Temple with a whip fashioned from cords (John 2:13-16). He displayed his nurturing side when he took a small child in his arms and portrayed the kind of humility he wanted from his followers (Mark 9:36-37). In the same way, God the Father feels and expresses a full array of emotions.

We also see God's willingness to engage our emotions in the book of Psalms. Inspired biblical authors wrote out their prayers as they grappled with their emotions. They express frustration, outrage and sadness with brutal honesty. Sometimes you feel like they're bordering on blasphemy when they take aim at God with their frustration. At other times, they summit the heights of joy and praise. God included the Psalms in Scripture to show us the kind of relationship he wants to have with us. When thoughts are swimming in our heads, God seeks to understand us. The Spirit "intercedes for us with groanings too deep for words" (Romans 8:26, NASB). God's Spirit can take our scrambled thoughts and translate them into clear prayers.

Willing to Discipline in Love

Parents in our culture rarely discipline their children. They won't deny their children what they want or set boundaries for them. They cave in to manipulation and temper tantrums. And when they attempt to discipline, it's out of anger or frustration.

Some of us grew up in a house like this. Our parents seldom said "no." As a result, we explode when we don't get our way. Perhaps we find ourselves trying to manipulate situations. We grate against authority like a rasp against a wood board. If people confront us, we cross our arms and glare at them. As a result, we find it hard to build close relationships.

According to biblical thinking, we should view sharing a word of correction with a friend or disciplining a child as a form of love.

The Bible teaches that we're born with a corrupt nature. The fall has thrown off our moral compass. What seems right or good often proves to be morally wrong and damaging. Therefore, we need God's loving discipline. The presence of God's discipline shows his love for us. Solomon urges his children, "Don't reject the Lord's discipline, and don't be upset when he corrects you. For the Lord corrects those he loves, just as a father corrects a child in whom he delights" (Proverbs 3:11-12, NLT). Discipline stands as a sign of our adoption. "If God doesn't discipline you as he does all of his children, it means that you are illegitimate and are not really his children at all" (Hebrews 12:8). "For," the author of Hebrews observes, "the LORD disciplines those he loves" (Hebrews 12:6).

Some of us underwent "discipline" growing up, but it was far from redemptive. Discipline meant Dad finally "had enough" and snapped on us. Love didn't motivate him to discipline; discipline was a way to vent frustration or anger. That's why discipline carries a lot of negative connotations for us. Many of us have responded by oversteering in the opposite direction. We're either too slow or entirely unwilling to speak a word of loving correction to those close to us. A few of us adopted the same pattern of harshness we saw from our father.

When God disciplines, he does so out of love. He never seeks to punish or vent his anger. He bore all of the wrath and punishment we deserve on the cross. Unlike our earthly fathers' flawed attempts to discipline, our heavenly Father never mixes anger with discipline. He also shows perfect timing, applying discipline exactly when we need it.

Patient

Scripture often describes God as displaying endless patience toward his people (Romans 2:4; 1 Peter 3:20; 2 Peter 3:15). New Testament writers picked a Greek word for patience that literally means "long suffering." To add a bit more texture to the meaning of this word, it describes one's ability to bear up under provocation.[1] When we turn back to the Old Testament, God reveals himself to Moses as "slow to anger" and "abounding in love" (Exodus 34:6). God's fuse burns slowly.

If you read the book of Revelation in one sitting, it's surprising how much God tolerates human rebellion. Even after God rains judgment upon the earth, the remaining survivors refuse to repent (Revelation 9:20-21). Reading the text feels like watching God walk a tightrope between tolerance and permissiveness as the final chapters careen toward the end of history. But Scripture explains why he endures so much rebellion: "He is patient...not wanting anyone to perish, but everyone to come to repentance" (2 Peter 3:9).

A number of us grew up with fathers who constantly seemed aggravated with us. Most of our interactions consisted of them barking at us to "stop" doing things. We felt like our presence irritated them. A few of us grew up with fathers who carried hair-trigger tempers. An outburst of anger could lead to verbal or even physical abuse.

On the other end of the spectrum, our heavenly Father patiently helps us through our constant moral failures. He gradually transforms us into the image of his Son. Our failures and setbacks never manage to surprise him. In fact, God often shows more forbearance toward us than we do toward ourselves.

Imparts Wisdom

Finally, good fathers impart wisdom to their children. Sadly, most of our parents' wisdom seems patterned after the world's wisdom. For example, our culture tells us that amassing lots of money and possessions will make us happy. Our world also tells us we should never commit to a marriage relationship unless we've slept with our partner.

---

[1] William Arndt, Frederick W. Danker, and Walter Bauer, *A Greek-English Lexicon of the New Testament and Other Early Christian Literature* (Chicago: University of Chicago Press, 2000), 612.

Even if our parents held a spiritual mindset, they may have avoided talking to us about certain topics. They might have stressed the importance of handling our money well, but sidestepped talking to us about sex. As a result, we've tried to stumble through this confusing area without any guidance. Fortunately, God speaks to every important area of life in his word. In particular, Proverbs speaks about practical topics like diligence, sexuality and finances. God fills the gaps in our understanding left by our earthly fathers.

Many of you can relate to one or more of the negative examples listed above. You live with the consequences of your earthly father's mistakes. But our heavenly Father more than makes up for your earthly father's flaws. He can repair the damage left by your father. For some of you, this assurance may help you take an important first step toward forgiving your earthly fathers.

Experiencing the Benefits of Adoption

Even if God has adopted you as his son or daughter, that doesn't guarantee you'll experience the benefits of adoption. Our corrupt human nature resists having to admit its need for God. That's why Jesus tells his disciples to become like little children if they want to be his followers. If you've ever been around small children, you're aware that they're not shy about asking for things. They never put on a front of self-reliance. They're shameless about their requests. In the same way, we need to develop a child-like trust in our heavenly Father. We should ask him to reveal our need for his wisdom and seek to find it.

For Further Discussion:

1. How should God's patience impact the way we relate to him and others? How should it impact the way we view our spiritual progress?
2. How should God's desire to engage us emotionally shape the way we pray?

THE SKILL OF LIVING

Where is the life we have lost in living? Where is the wisdom we have lost in knowledge? Where is the knowledge we have lost in information?

T.S. Eliot[1]

We're drowning in information, yet thirsting for wisdom. We possess more information now than at any other time in human history, all available at the click of a button. But we don't appear any wiser because of our privilege. Warren Wiersbe puts it best when he says,

> We're living in the "information age," but we certainly aren't living in the "age of wisdom." Many people who are wizards with their computers seem to be amateurs when it comes to making a success out of their lives. Computers can store data and obey signals, but they can't give us the ability to use that knowledge wisely. What's needed today is wisdom.[2]

Our world contains many brilliant and extremely knowledgeable people. Yet, their personal lives lay in ruins. They can build a successful business, but they can't seem to build successful relationships. They can develop complex software, but they can't develop a simple budget and stay out of debt. We live in both a feast of information and a famine of wisdom.

Knowledge differs greatly from wisdom. Today we passively consume information as our devices bombard us with it. But we must actively seek wisdom, which conceals itself from the proud

---

[1] Excerpt from Part II of "Choruses from 'The Rock'" in *Collected Poems 1909-1962* by T.S. Eliot.

[2] Warren Wiersbe, *Be Skillful (Proverbs): God's Guidebook to Wise Living* (Colorado Springs, CO: David C. Cook, 2009), 7.

(Proverbs 1:6). In Proverbs, Wisdom personified speaks and tells us, "Blessed is the man who listens to me, watching daily at my doors, waiting at my doorway" (Proverbs 8:34).

What is wisdom?

The first two lines of Proverbs state why Solomon wrote and collected these proverbs. "Their purpose is to teach people wisdom and discipline, to help them understand the insights of the wise" (Proverbs 1:2, NLT). In our day, to "understand" something denotes a cognitive process. You commit it to memory, you comprehend it and you analyze it. But the Hebrew word for *understanding* travels beyond the borders of mere intellect. It means applying what you know and letting it impact your life.[3]

The Old Testament uses the Hebrew word *wisdom* (*hokmah*) to describe a skill or craft. For instance, God gave Moses these instructions, "Tell all the skilled [*hokmah*] men to whom I have given wisdom [*hokmah*]...that they are to make garments for Aaron...so he may serve me as priest" (Exodus 28:3). The text uses the adjective form of this word to refer to the "skilled men." These seamsters possessed the skill (*hokmah*) to harvest flax, weave it into linen and sew it into garments.

In another Old Testament example, God called Moses to assemble craftsmen to construct the Tent of Meeting. So "Moses summoned...every skilled person to whom the LORD had given ability and who was willing to come and do the work" (Exodus 36:2, NET). These men possessed the skill (*hokmah*) of finished carpentry and metalwork. They could take a solid block of gold and hammer ornate candelabras. Or they could take a thin-film coating of gold and lay it on wooden furniture.

---

[3] According to the *Theological Workbook of the Old Testament*, 'The verb refers to knowledge which is superior to the mere gathering of data...[The verb] can also mean "understanding" in the sense of ability (e.g. Esau as a skilful hunter).' R. Laird Harris, Gleason L. Archer Jr., and Bruce K. Waltke, eds. *Theological Wordbook of the Old Testament* (Chicago: Moody Press, 1999), 103.

A few years ago, I got my hands on an old steel bike frame. After months of research, I stumbled across a local bike frame builder who restores bikes. I drove an hour away to his shop, which was in the middle of nowhere. When I arrived, I pulled into a long driveway leading to a house. I knocked on the door, but no one answered. I wasn't even sure if I was at the right place. Confused, I looked around the property and saw faint tire marks leading toward the back of the house.

Against my better judgment, I followed the tracks to a large cement-block building nestled in the woods. Outside stood an old ATV, some rusting steel tubes and other debris scattered around the entrance. I slowly turned the doorknob and peeked into the building. Inside was a heavyset man draped in a Notre Dame sweatshirt, shot through with holes. He was clutching a two-liter bottle of Diet Coke. He peered at me as he took a gulp from his two-liter. "May I help you?" he asked.

As I looked around his shop, the flickering fluorescent lights revealed metal working equipment jammed into every corner. His shop smelled like your hand after digging through a bowl of pennies.

Despite his rough exterior, he possessed extensive knowledge about bikes. I asked him what size seatpost I needed for my bike because I couldn't get one to fit. He narrowed his eyes and looked at my frame. He replied, "Columbus SLX tubing always takes a 27.2mm seatpost. The reason your seatpost won't fit in there," he said, grabbing the frame from my hands, "is because the seatpost collar is pinched." He picked up a screwdriver and wedged it between the ears of my seatpost collar, prying them apart. Then he flipped the frame upside down and reamed it out with one of his tools. He took a seatpost lying around and it slid right into the seat tube.

You could say this guy possessed the *hokmah* of frame building. His mind contained vast knowledge about the properties of steel. He could predict how steel tubes would respond under the stress and load of a cyclist mashing on the pedals. But his knowledge went beyond theory. He could manipulate steel by cutting, shaping and welding it.

In the same way, wisdom describes the skill of living. It points to the ability to predict the outcome of a situation. Certain actions yield certain results. And the wise person can visualize the domino effect a decision may trigger. "Wise people think before they act; fools don't—and even brag about their foolishness" (Proverbs 13:16, NLT). But wisdom moves beyond the confines of head knowledge. Wise people practically apply their knowledge. For example, a wise woman watches the ant labor during summer in preparation for winter. Then she mimics its behavior by working hard to lay aside enough for leaner times (Proverbs 6:6-8). Or, a wise man sees that the same words can yield two completely different responses depending on the situation. So he chooses to speak in some and keep his mouth shut in others (Proverbs 26:4-5).

So on one level, *hokmah* refers to the skill of living. But on a more profound level, it refers to understanding the ways things work in the world.

Laws of Observation

Before their famous first flight, the Wright brothers owned a bicycle shop in Dayton, Ohio. Orville and Wilbur took the profits from their business and financed their obsession with aviation. During business hours, they wrenched on and sold bikes at their shop. After hours, they climbed to the second floor of their bike shop where they had constructed a primitive wind tunnel. They spent late nights testing different wing shapes and finally discovered the basic principles of lift. The Wright brothers discerned the created order through trial, error and observation. Yet, most people picture the Wright brothers bringing their prototype to the windy beaches at Kitty Hawk, North Carolina, and crossing their fingers. In reality, they *knew* their plane would fly.[4] Likewise, wisdom refers to a working knowledge about the created order. Solomon declares, "By wisdom the Lord laid the earth's

---

[4] This analogy came from Bruce Waltke's lectures on Proverbs.

foundations, by understanding he set the heavens in place" (Proverbs 3:19). The wise person looks at the created order and sees the marks of God's wisdom. That's why the book of Proverbs refers to wisdom as a "law" (Proverbs 1:8, 3:1, 13:14).[5]

In science, a law refers to a statement based on the repeated observation of a natural occurrence. The wise man uses the word "law" in the same way scientists talk about a natural law. If you disregard the law of gravity and take a step off a 10-story building, you may experience a thrill on the way down. But the result will prove fatal. In the same way, disobeying the wise man's wisdom may lead to ruin. "There is a way that seems right to a man, but in the end it leads to death" (Proverbs 14:12).

Whereas Moses obtained his revelation through an encounter with God, the wise man obtains revelation through observing God's created order. The Holy Spirit moved the authors of Proverbs to speak for God. That's what sets the book of Proverbs apart from other proverbs. It separates God's revelation from mere human observation. For example, the ancient Epicurean philosopher would say, "Eat, drink and be merry, because tomorrow we die." He saw death as the final destination. So he concludes, "We should maximize our pleasure." On the other hand, the wise man says, "Eat, drink, and be merry, for it is the gift of God" (Ecclesiastes 3:13, NASB). The wise man looks at death, but through the filter of faith.

Gaining Wisdom from Proverbs

The Hebrew word proverb means "a comparison." At times, they appear as sharp and sometimes humorous similes. For example, "As a door swings back and forth on its hinges, so the lazy person turns over in bed (Proverbs 26:14, NLT). Or a proverb may show up as a full-grown allegory. In Ezekiel 17, the prophet depicts God as an eagle who plants a vine in fertile soil.

---

[5] Solomon exhorts his children, "Listen, my son, to your father's instruction and do not forsake your mother's teaching" (Proverbs 1:8). Solomon uses the Hebrew word *torah* for "teaching."

The Proverbs serve as axioms for living. The wise man fashions a proverb from experience and observation. Like forming a bouillon cube from broth, the wise man reduces several lifetimes of observation into one short saying. Spanish novelist Cervantes defines a proverb as "a short sentence based on long experience."

A proverb describes a clever, yet practical saying meant to stick in your mind. They're pithy statements pregnant with meaning. Even when a proverb lodges itself into your mind, its meaning often remains locked. Only further reflection unlatches it.

Our culture contains its own set of proverbs, although we don't call them proverbs. We just call them "sayings." Here are a few:

"The early bird gets the worm."

This proverb teaches that diligent people seize opportunities, thus gaining an advantage over others.

"Where there is smoke, there is fire."

This teaches that rumors are often rooted in some truth.

"Don't judge a book by its cover."

You shouldn't form an opinion about someone based on his or her outward appearance.

"A man who lives in a glass house should change his clothes in the basement."

When you live in the public eye, take care to hide what you don't want people to see.

"A peacock that sits on its tail is just another turkey."

I'm not sure what that one means.

Although our modern sayings resemble the Proverbs, biblical wisdom requires special treatment. If we don't use the right tools for interpreting Proverbs, we'll end up with the wrong interpretation.

Reading Proverbs

Proverbs don't always make sense in their context. The authors didn't write in a linear fashion. As a result, the content in the book of Proverbs frequently jumps around. One moment, Solomon might be giving an extended metaphor about wisdom; the next, he's criticizing the mocker for disdaining correction (9:1-9). In one breath, he may talk both about the foolishness of a sluggard and the power of speech (10:26, 31). Therefore, we must view each topic as a constellation of ideas scattered throughout the book.

Also, the proverbs give balance to each other. For instance, many "health and wealth" teachers argue that God wants to bless you with riches and good health. And they could easily fortify their position by quoting from the Proverbs. For example, they often cite Proverbs 10:15, "The rich man's wealth is his fortress" (NASB). But the book of Proverbs also says,

> Do not weary yourself to gain wealth, cease from your consideration *of it.* When you set your eyes on it, it is gone. For *wealth* certainly makes itself wings like an eagle that flies *toward* the heavens. (23:4-5, NASB)

So to obtain a clear picture of what the Proverbs say on a certain topic, we need to collect all of the proverbs on that topic. Then we need to lay them all out, stand back and evaluate them as a whole.

At times, a proverb may describe a cause-and-effect relationship it doesn't endorse. To use the example above, the wise man didn't intend to promote materialism when he wrote Proverbs 10:15. He simply confronts us with a brute fact. The rich leverage their wealth to wiggle their way out of trouble. Their riches provide a hedge of protection. But the wise man sees that wealth provides limited protection. Beyond this life, "Wealth is worthless in the day of wrath, but righteousness delivers from death" (Proverbs 11:4).

Also, we shouldn't view proverbs as precise statements that hold true in every situation. We shouldn't treat them as promises. Take the case of Proverbs 17:17, "A friend loves at all times." But experience tells us that sometimes even the closest friends disagree. Or Proverbs 15:1, "A gentle answer turns away wrath." But we will run into cases where a calm response will trigger someone's anger.

The Proverbs offer us practical advice. They teach us how to relate to our spouse and children. They show us how to treat our friends. The Proverbs also instruct us about the way we use our words. In fact, God spills more ink about the way we use our words than any other topic in Proverbs. Our words can either save us or entrap us (12:13). They can impart life or claim it (18:21). The Proverbs also speak to functional aspects of life, such as handling money and the dangers of lending to friends.

Though understanding Proverbs requires interpretive skill, it also requires the right attitude. To squeeze the most wisdom from Proverbs, we need what the Bible calls the "fear of the Lord."

Fear of the Lord

The opening page of Proverbs hands us its thesis statement, "The fear of the LORD is the beginning of knowledge; fools despise wisdom and instruction" (1:7). The book of Proverbs aims to cultivate the fear of the Lord in us.

Now when we hear the term "fear of the Lord" our minds instantly jump to God's judgment. But the fear of the Lord contains a wide range of meaning. It includes "reverence," "awe," "devotion," or "an eagerness to listen." Warren Wiersbe defines it this way, "It's not the servile fear of the slave before the master, but the reverential and respectful fear of the child before the parent."[6] Solomon gives us a more complete definition in Proverbs 3:5-7:

> Trust in the LORD with all your heart and do not lean on your own understanding. In all your ways acknowledge Him, and He will make your paths straight. Do not be wise in your own eyes; fear the LORD and turn away from evil.

Like turning a gemstone in sunlight, Solomon presents us with several facets of the fear of the Lord. Let's evaluate each.

"Trust in the Lord"

Scripture hoists faith onto its shoulders as one of the most important qualities a Christian can possess. But when most people in our culture hear the word "faith," they equate it with either

---

[6] Wiersbe, *Be Skillful*, 24.

wishful thinking or blind faith. Biblical faith grounds itself in truth. Hebrews 11:1 provides us with a working definition of faith: "Faith is being sure of what we hope for and certain of what we do not see." It describes more than just an intellectual belief (i.e., belief that Abraham Lincoln existed). It also describes placing our trust in what God says.

When I first entered college, I pursued an engineering degree. The college of engineering required three physics classes to gain acceptance into the major. So I scheduled an early morning physics class my freshman year. One day, I recall sitting in a large lecture hall filled with hundreds of students as our professor was explaining how gravity acts on a pendulum. "Gravity" he said, "exerts a downward force on the mass of a pendulum." He continued, "Therefore, a pendulum loses energy each time it completes a cycle." The lecture hall looked like an oil field, as students' heads would nod off and spring back up.

In the middle of the lecture, our professor lowered a 20-lb bowling ball attached to the three-story ceiling of the lecture hall. Students sat up in their chairs. The bowling ball stopped six inches from the ground. My professor bent over, grabbed the bowling ball and started walking it backward toward the corner of the room. He pressed his back against the corner and pinned his head to it. Then, he took the bowling ball and touched it to his chin. With labored breathing he asked, "How many of you believe this bowling ball will swing back and crush my face?" He didn't wait for a response. He just let go.

The bowling ball screamed toward the other side of the room and then started to slow. It stood motionless when it reached the peak of its amplitude and started to swing back. As it gained more momentum, some students let out a gasp. As the ball swung toward our professor, it froze an inch from his face.

It struck me that this was an illustration of biblical faith. My professor not only held an intellectual belief in the law of gravity, he also placed his personal trust in it. In the same way, fearing the Lord means more than holding a belief in God's existence. It means placing our trust in him.

"Lean not on your own understanding"

Most people act as if they know what's best. But their lives make it clear that they're confused. By comparison, the wise person sees her need for input. She feels wary about leaning on her intuitions and feelings. Proverbs 12:15 captures this perfectly, "The way of a fool seems right to him, but a wise man listens to advice."

According to the Bible, we possess a fallen nature. Sin clouds our minds. Selfishness shapes our values and desires. Therefore, we're unable to see things clearly. That's why Solomon warns us, "Do not be wise in your own eyes." Instead, he directs us to "fear the Lord."

The fear of the Lord cannot thrive without humility. Humility describes holding a realistic view of yourself. It avoids either extreme of seeing yourself as worthless or viewing yourself more highly than you ought. Humility allows you to see your need for God's wisdom.

"In all your ways acknowledge him"

The Hebrew word for "acknowledge" carries a wider range of meaning than our word. It embraces the idea of showing "an awareness of" and "fellowship with" someone. So the fear of the Lord includes relating to him in a personal way.

Often, we take a mechanistic approach to our relationship with God. We put in our good works and devotion and wait for him to dispense blessing and guidance. But we don't relate to him as our Father.

Also, the fear of the Lord requires us to acknowledge him in *every* area of our lives. Many of us have sealed off areas of our life, permitting God restricted access. But the fear of the Lord demands us to tear down these partitions and authorize him to give us input in all areas. For example, wise people don't separate their functional life from their spiritual life. They see how decisions related to career advancement may impact their spiritual life. Or that spiritual maturity requires diligence. That's why Proverbs covers a variety of practical topics. God shows as much concern about how much overtime we spend at the office as he does how much we pray.

The Fool

Solomon contrasts the fear of the Lord with fools who "despise wisdom and instruction" (Proverbs 1:7). The Proverbs don't use the term "fool" to describe a friend who uses slapstick humor to get laughs. The term contains moral overtones. It describes someone who ignores or disdains God's wisdom.

The fool appears in the book of Proverbs under various identities. Proverbs lists five types of fools, all with varying degrees of hard-heartedness.[7] In Proverbs 1:7, Solomon refers to the type of fool that displays moral defiance and a flippant attitude towards God. Most notable, this fool shows an unwillingness to listen. If he gets an idea in his head, nothing will stop him. It's best just to give him a wide berth. "Better to meet a bear robbed of her cubs than a fool in his folly" (Proverbs 17:12).

But a condition like this doesn't develop overnight. You don't wake up one morning, look in the mirror and see that you've turned into a fool. It takes place gradually. This kind of foolishness can be nearly impossible to eradicate unless treated early. The wise man describes this advanced case of foolishness, "Though you pound a fool in a mortar with a pestle...*yet* his foolishness will not depart from him" (Proverbs 27:22, NASB).

For this reason, Solomon refers to proverbs as "riddles" (Proverbs 1:6). They conceal themselves from some and reveal themselves to others. Only a certain attitude can unlock their meaning. You could say the same thing about God's word in general. When the 72 disciples returned from their mission, Jesus prayed, "O Father, Lord of heaven and earth, thank you for hiding these things from those who think themselves wise and clever, and for revealing them to the childlike" (Luke 10:21, NLT). Proverbs

---

[7] For a concise discussion on the five types of fool in Proverbs, see Derek Kidner, *Proverbs: An Introduction and Commentary*. Vol. 17. Tyndale Old Testament Commentaries. (Downers Grove, IL: InterVarsity Press, 1964), 37.

hides its wisdom from the proud and reveals it to the humble. If we want to get the most out of Proverbs we need to read it with a spirit of humility.

Sadly, some of us resonate with this description of the fool. Like me, you may not have grown up with the fear of the Lord. Perhaps your upbringing didn't include contact with many Christians. Maybe your parents never applied loving discipline in your home. Whatever led to your condition, it's not too late to turn things around. Wisdom awaits you, if you admit your need for God's input. And he promises to lavish wisdom upon those who ask for it (James 1:5).

For Further Discussion:

1. What are some of the differences between wisdom and knowledge?
2. What are some signs that we're leaning on human wisdom rather than God's wisdom?
3. Aside from devoting your entire life to God, how can we acknowledge God in all our ways?

THE SLUGGARD

def. [**sluhg**-erd] n. "a person who is habitually inactive or lazy"

The book of Proverbs depicts the life of a sluggard as a tragic comedy, filled with pathetic stories of laziness and outrageous excuses. Chronic laziness contradicts our design. It strips us of our humanity and reduces us down to our animal instincts.

God's nature compels him to work. Jesus defended healing a paralyzed man on the Sabbath by saying, "My Father is always working, and so am I" (John 5:17). Our world speaks of God's diligence. The author of Hebrews tells us, "Through the Son [God] created the universe...and he sustains everything by the mighty power of his command" (Hebrews 3:1). The universe would collapse if God didn't sustain it. Even God's creation exhibits his diligence, "Go to the ant, you sluggard; consider its ways and be wise! It has no commander, no overseer or ruler, yet it stores its provisions in summer and gathers its food at harvest" (Proverbs 6:6-8).

Since God fashioned us in his image, he hardwired diligence into our framework. Therefore, we violate our design when we live as a sluggard. Let's examine the life of a sluggard.

The Life of a Sluggard

Inactivity. Sluggards never get enough rest. According to Derek Kidner, "He's more than anchored to his bed, he is hinged to it."[1] The wise man observes, "As a door swings back and forth on its hinges, so the lazy person turns over in bed." (Proverbs 26:14, NLT). If you see a sluggard lying in bed, you're observing him in his natural habitat. He stirs as if to get up, but he's just turning over to hit the snooze button. By comparison, hard work rewards the diligent with a sound night's sleep.

---

[1] Derek Kidner, *Proverbs: An Introduction and Commentary.* Vol. 17. Tyndale Old Testament Commentaries (Downers Grove, IL: InterVarsity Press, 1964), 39.

The constant need for rest isn't just a feature of the sluggard's nature. It develops when he constantly gives in to laziness. Proverbs 6:9-10 describes the outcome of chronic inactivity, "How long will you lie there, you sluggard? When will you get up from your sleep?

A little sleep...

A little slumber...

A little folding of the hands to rest

And poverty will come on you like a bandit and scarcity like an armed man."

Derek Kidner captures the somewhat humorous and altogether pathetic condition of the sluggard:

When we ask the sluggard 'How long ...?' 'When ...?' we are being too definite for him. He doesn't know. All he knows is his delicious drowsiness; all he asks is a little respite: 'a little...a little...a little...' He does not commit himself to a refusal, but deceives himself by the smallness of his surrenders. So, by inches and minutes, his opportunity slips away.[2]

You don't just wake up one morning, look in the mirror and discover that you're a sluggard.[3] It's a slow, subtle process, which suddenly ends in tragedy. Ronald Sailer describes it this way, "Laziness could run a competitive race for the most underrated sin...Quietly it anesthetizes its victim into a lifeless stupor that ends in hunger, bondage and death."[4]

Depression. Excessive sleep and chronic fatigue often point to depression. But in the sluggard's case, it's the reverse. His depression stems from excessive sleep and chronic laziness. Do you ever wonder what thoughts swim around in the sluggard's head as he lays on the couch? The wise person tells us, "The soul of the

---

[2] Ibid.

[3] Ibid., 40.

[4] Ronald Sailler and David Wyrtzen, *The Practice of Wisdom* (Chicago: Moody, 1992), 82.

sluggard craves and gets nothing, but the desires of the diligent are fully satisfied" (Proverbs 13:4). The sluggard lusts after things he doesn't have. He lives in an imaginary world. No wonder, you find most sluggards connected to a video game console, grappling with pornography addiction, or compulsively eating.

Although sluggards thirst for the things they want, they "get nothing." Depression eats away at them. And over time, it destroys their life. "The sluggard's craving will be the death of him, because his hands refuse to work. All day long he craves for more..." (Proverbs 21:25-26). Sluggards daydream about the kind of life they want instead of working for it. You'll see them gesticulating with excitement as they describe some grandiose plan that will make them successful. But it never happens. It just ends up in the bin of ideas that never get accomplished.

Financial Difficulty. Laziness can inflict the sluggard with more than just depression. It can ruin him financially (his "craving will be the death of him") and imprison him spiritually ("All day long he craves for more").[5]

Proverbs places the sluggard and the diligent side by side to highlight two different outcomes. Proverbs 10:4 states, "Lazy hands make a man poor, but diligent hands bring wealth" (Proverbs 10:4). And Proverbs 14:23 says, "Work brings profit, but mere talk leads to poverty." Of course, the wise person isn't suggesting that all poverty stems from laziness. In an earlier chapter ("The Skill of Living"), we explained that proverbs represent general statements about the world. The wise person sees that injustice and corruption sweep away what little the poor possess. But as a rule, the hardworking don't fall into poverty. They turn a profit and expand their wealth. By contrast, the fool merely talks about how they'll make money (Proverbs 12:11). But a lack of follow-through lands them in financial disaster.

The sluggard's bills pile up as she lounges around the house. When you ask her when she plans to pay her portion of the bills,

---

[5] Kidner, *Proverbs*, 137.

she barely looks up from the screen to which she's glued her eyes. She huffs as if you were interrupting something important. "Don't worry, I'll get it to you," she insists. But a week passes and she still hasn't coughed up the money.

Lying Excuses. The sluggard's mouth pours out excuses: "The check should be coming in the mail today," "Work messed up my direct deposit," "I've been really busy, I'll get it to you tomorrow." The sluggard shows unlimited creativity when it comes to fabricating excuses. Proverbs 26:13 furnishes us with one, "The sluggard says, 'There is a lion in the road, a fierce lion roaming the streets!'" To put it in our terms, when you ask a sluggard, "Why aren't you putting out applications for a job?" they say, "Didn't you hear? A ferocious snow leopard escaped from the zoo. It's dangerous out there! I'm gonna stay here and finish my family-size box of Cap'n Crunch cereal." As one famous Christian teacher put it, "An excuse is a skin of reason stuffed with a lie."[6] People who are good at giving excuses are rarely good at doing anything else.

Sluggards also put off the appearance of busyness even though they never get anything done. They spring to action when their boss appears, pretending they've been working the whole time. But as soon as the boss leaves the room, they resume their inactivity.

Arrogance. Sluggards vaunt themselves as experts of any topic of conversation. They can't resist asserting their opinions. Proverbs 26:16 says, "Lazy people consider themselves smarter than seven wise counselors" (NLT). That's how sluggards justify doing less. They convince themselves that they're smarter. That's why they don't have to try as hard. Wiersbe depicts the sluggard's hubris:

> He lives in a fantasy world that prevents him from being a useful part of the real world, but he can tell everybody else what to do. He's never succeeded at anything in his own life, but he can tell others how to succeed.[7]

---

[6] Billy Sunday

[7] Wiersbe, *Be Skillful*, 86.

Sluggards are quick to sign up for something, but slow to get started. They're always putting things off until the last minute. People constantly have to remind them of the rapidly approaching deadline.

On the rare occasion that a sluggard exerts some effort to begin a task, the task proves too much and the impulse dies. Solomon portrays the sluggard's lack of follow-through this way: "The sluggard plunges his hand in the dish; he is too lazy to bring it back to his mouth" (Proverbs 26:15, NET). Can you imagine someone raising a spoonful of soup, but failing to cover the distance from the bowl to his or her mouth? Sluggards leave behind unfinished construction sites, half-written papers for school and a mess for others to clean. They never finish things because they underestimate how much time it will take. And they overestimate their ability to get it done. But there's more at stake than growing hungry and getting cold.

Dangers of Chronic Laziness

Debt eventually subjugates the sluggard. "A sluggard does not plow in season; so at harvest time he looks but finds nothing" (Proverbs 20:4). Laziness has left the sluggard with nothing. Consequently, he mooches off those around him. In fact, he walks around with a sense of entitlement, as if people owe him something. But when friends and family get fed up and cut him off financially, he resorts to selling himself to those willing to lend him money. Year after year, mounting debt slowly buries the sluggard alive until the lender has confiscated the sluggard's freedom. "Diligent hands will rule, but laziness ends in slave labor" (Proverbs 12:24). The sluggard toils just to pay off the interest on his debt. Wiersbe summarizes this thought when he says, "The 'easy life' of leisure turns out to be very costly as the sluggard exchanges his pillow for a plow and has to work off his debts."[8]

To a sluggard, everything boils down to one simple calculation: How much suffering am I willing to endure before I exert some

---

[8] Ibid., 87.

effort? Some translations of the Bible use the world "sloth" in place of sluggard, and for good reason. Sloths move only when it's necessary. Even when they begin to move, you won't find a sloth breaking any land-speed records. Sloths move at a rate of 10 feet per minute.[9]

My close friend spent a good part of her childhood living in the Amazon jungle of Brazil. Like any good Amazonian, she owned a pet sloth. Each day, she and her brother would watch their pet sloth inch its way up a 15 foot tree in their backyard. It took most of the day for it to reach the canopy. The sloth would fill its stomach and then, instead of starting its descent, it would just let go. From time to time, they would hear a crash coming from their backyard. They would look out their window and see their sloth lying on the concrete patio beneath the tree. The first time they heard a crash, they ran outside to see what happened. Tears rolled down their cheeks as they stood over their motionless sloth. But two minutes later, it reanimated and slowly climbed back up the tree. Like the sloth, many sluggards calculate effort using a suffering-to-exertion ratio. They ask themselves, "How much suffering am I willing to endure, before I exert some effort?"

Sluggards also act as an irritant to whomever works with them. Proverbs 10:26 states, "As vinegar to the teeth and smoke to the eyes, so is a sluggard to those who send him." "Vinegar to the teeth" describes the sharp pain you feel when you bite into something acidic with sensitive teeth. "Smoke to the eyes," refers to the sting of smoke drifting into your eyes while sitting by a campfire. This proverb teaches that putting a sluggard to work can be more of a nuisance than a help. He'll probably mess up the job you sent him to do. Or he'll leave it unfinished. If he manages to finish, you'll end up redoing it because he's done such a poor job.

For many years, I struggled with laziness. For example, I skipped most of classes during my first year of college. On cold

---

[9] M. Goffart, "Function and Form in the Sloth" in *International Series of Monographs in Pure and Applied Biology*, vol. 34 (Oxford: Pergamon Press, 1971), 94–95.

winter mornings, I'd lie in bed and ask myself, "Why should I make the trek through four inches of snow, just to hear what I can read from the textbook?" When midterms came, I'd scramble to cram for my exams. As a result, I failed a few classes during my first year of college.

Causes of Laziness

What drives the sluggard's way of life? How does someone become a sluggard? Several reasons come to mind.

For some of us, no one ever instilled in us the value of hard work. No one modeled it for us. Our parents never provided structure at home. After school, we watched countless hours of TV and immersed ourselves in social media and videogames. As a result, we're struggling to break free from this pattern of laziness.

My father and mother immigrated to the United States in the early 1960s. During that time, tens of thousands of Filipinos flooded the United States looking for a better life. My dad did accounting for a manufacturing company. Every morning, I watched him put on a collared shirt and tie before starting his hour-long commute before the sun rose. He'd pore through accounting books on the weekends, eager to sharpen his skills. Years of watching him do this made a deep impression on me. His example showed me the dignity of doing your job well and providing for your family. I'll admit I didn't follow his example right away. But in the long run, I came back to it.

Secondly, sluggards don't feel like they need to answer to anyone. They don't see their lives as something loaned to them. They live as owners not stewards. In Matthew 25, Jesus tells his disciples a parable about a wealthy landowner who planned on taking a trip to a distant country. Before he left, he gathered his three servants together and entrusted each of them with a large sum of money. To the first, he gave five talents. To the second, he gave two. And to the last servant, he gave just one talent.

Today, we connect the word "talent" with someone's gifting. We would say, "She possesses creative talent." But in New Testament times, people used talent to describe a unit of weight (roughly 80 lbs.). Now Matthew doesn't clarify if Jesus was talking about a talent of gold or silver. Either way, he was describing a large sum of money.[10] Even the servant who managed just one talent was handling a lot of money.

Jesus tells us the servants with five and two talents "went out immediately" and invested their money (25:16). Their work was marked with urgency and purpose. They took what the landowner gave them and doubled it. But the servant with one talent went a different direction. He went out to a field, dug a hole and buried his talent.

Years pass and the wealthy landowner returned unannounced. He summoned his three servants to settle accounts. Rubbing his hands together, he asked the first one, "What did you do with my five talents?" The servant smiled, "I doubled your money." The wealthy landowner exclaimed, "Well done!" He responded the same way to the second servant who also doubled his money.

"And what about you?" he said to the last servant. The servant replied, "I know you're a ruthless business man, harvesting from fields you never planted. Out of fear, I hid your money. Here's every penny of it." After the servant finished speaking, the wealthy landowner sat silent.

Suddenly, the wealthy landowner erupted, "You wicked, lazy servant! You're familiar with how I do business; that I harvest crops from fields I don't own. If you were afraid of me, why didn't you put my money in the bank so that I would at least earn some interest?" Then, he commanded one of his servants, "Seize the talent from this worthless servant and throw him into the outer darkness."

What was this servant guilty of doing? Did he steal money from the landowner? Did he embezzle the money he was given? No. He

---

[10] Matthew uses the Greek word *argūrion*, which we translate "money." The chemical element AG (silver on the Periodic table) comes from the Latin translation of this word. If Jesus was referring to a talent of silver, it would be worth $650,000 today.

didn't do any of these things. According to Jesus, he was guilty of doing nothing. Most people hold that God judges us for the bad things we do. But according to the Bible, we're also liable for failing to do the good we ought to do (James 4:17).

Let me offer a few observations about this parable. First, the servant falsely accuses his master of unethical behavior. In Jesus' parable, the master represents God. Instead of defending himself, the wealthy landowner brilliantly uses the servant's *own* reasoning against him. "If you were afraid of misplacing my money, then why didn't you put it in the bank and earn some interest?" Lying excuses dribble out of the sluggard's mouth. A sluggard will distort the truth and even run someone's reputation through the mud to justify his own inaction.

Second, the servant didn't *really* view his master as a "hard man." In fact, it was just the opposite. The servant viewed him as soft. He must have said to himself, "My boss has been gone a long time. What's the likelihood that he's even coming back? Even if he does, what's he going to do anyway?" Sluggards don't see themselves as stewards; they see themselves as owners. That's how they justify wasting their lives. But God promises he will return one day to settle accounts. Luckily, no one who has forged a relationship with God through Christ will stand under his judgment. Yet, we will still stand before him to explain what we did with our lives. He will reward those who were faithful. And those who squandered their lives will experience loss.

Third, it's possible the servant was upset the landowner gave him a smaller amount of money. Obviously, we're entering the realm of speculation. But sluggards typically make excuses like this to justify their laziness. "If only I were smarter, then I'd try harder in school," they say. Or, "She makes it look so easy. There's no way I could do that." But it's not a matter of how much God has given you; it's a matter of what you *do* with what he has given you.

Deliverance from Laziness

If you want to gain freedom from laziness, start by giving your life to God. This attacks the roots of laziness in your life. Regimenting your time or upbraiding yourself will only produce superficial change. Each time you hand over a new area of your life to God, you begin to see things differently. You no longer see yourself as the owner of your life; you see it as on loan to you. You start living life as though you'll have to give an account; not in servile fear, but with eagerness to please your heavenly Father. Once you start to see your life this way, you won't seek to do the bare minimum. You won't try to do just enough to keep people off your back. Instead, you'll have an inward drive to buy up the limited time you have on earth. That's how I experienced deliverance from laziness.

Early on in my Christian life, I dedicated myself to serving God. I set out to make my life count for Christ. Yet, my functional life lagged behind. Eventually, my indolence started to interfere with my goal to serve Christ. When I started failing classes, I lost a certain amount of credibility with the people I was trying to influence spiritually. That's what finally convinced me to take this area of my life seriously.

Secondly, learn from the fate of the sluggard. The wise person observes,

> I passed by the field of the sluggard and by the vineyard of the man lacking sense, and behold, it was completely overgrown with thistles; its surface was covered with nettles, and its stone wall was broken down. When I saw, I reflected upon it; I looked, *and* received instruction. 'A little sleep, a little slumber, a little folding of the hands to rest,' then your poverty will come *as* a robber and your want like an armed man. (Proverbs 24:30-34, NASB)

If the book of Proverbs teaches us anything, it's that wise people learn from others' mistakes. You don't have to suffer the fate of a sluggard to see that laziness ruins people's lives.

Some of you might feel like laziness has a stranglehold on you. If you're ready to see some victory, take the first step of submitting yourself to God's loving discipline. The moment you received Christ, God committed himself to working gradual change in your life (Philippians 1:6). But he requires you to cooperate. Up to this point, you may have thrown away amazing opportunities. After years of freeloading, you may have damaged relationships with family members and close friends. How much longer will you allow laziness to ravage your life? Turn to God and ask him to change you. Ask him to break you of your laziness. It's the only way you're going to see change.

Finally, take small steps toward becoming diligent. People who struggle with laziness size up difficult tasks and wave them off as impossible. Diligent people can break them down into small, manageable parts. Doing this will make any task feel less overwhelming. You may fail the first few times you try. But, you won't find anything worthwhile easy to accomplish. Keep working at it until you start getting some traction. Sooner or later, you'll accomplish what you've set out to do. String together a few of these victories and you'll start to get a taste for the satisfaction of hard work.

And to those of us who have a sluggard in our life, we must firmly apply God's loving discipline. We need to show strength and speak God's truth in love. But God's loving discipline implies more than talking. Sometimes it requires taking a stand. If they're unwilling to work, refuse to pay their bills or give them money. Don't enable their life of laziness. It will only hurt them long-term. It's difficult to say 'no' to someone you love, especially if they find themselves in trouble. But you need to do what's best for them, even if it makes them angry. You need to put your confidence in God's hands to repair their life (2 Thessalonians 3:10).

For Further Discussion:

1. Why do you think God speaks so strongly against laziness?
2. What are other steps you could take to overcome chronic laziness?

WORDS AT THEIR WORST

The English novelist Edward Lytton coined the famous statement, "The pen is mightier than the sword." History provides us with countless examples of its truth. For example, Karl Marx's *Communist Manifesto* sparked a revolution that claimed the lives of over 50 million people in just 40 years. According to Warren Wiersbe, "for every word in Hitler's book *Mein Kampf*, 125 people died in World War II."

The Power of God's Word

The biblical account of creation stands in sharp contrast to other ancient creation stories. Often these narratives depict a god or several gods constructing the universe using human methods. The gods give shape to the universe by swinging hammers and pounding chisels. And they use existing materials to build the universe. These creation accounts resemble something ancient man conceived.

By contrast, the God of the Bible creates by what Christian scholars call divine *fiat*. When he decrees something ("let there be..."), it pops into existence ("and there was..."). Psalm 33:6 and 9 declare, "The Lord merely spoke, and the heavens were created. He breathed the word, and all the stars were born. For when he spoke, the world began!"

The opening lines of the Bible tell us the earth sat "formless and void" until God spoke, "Let there be light!" and light appeared (Genesis 1:2-3). Thus, according to the biblical account, the world appeared at God's command.

Scripture teaches that God executes his will through his word. In Isaiah 55:9-11, God describes the confidence he places in his word to carry out his purposes:

For as the heavens are higher than the earth, so are My ways higher than your ways and My thoughts than your thoughts. For as the rain and the snow come down from heaven, and do not return there without watering the earth...So will My word be which goes forth from My mouth; it will not return to Me empty, without accomplishing what I desire, and without succeeding in the matter for which I sent it. (NASB)

Passages like this argue against the view that cultural bias blocks us from accessing the Bible's original meaning. If God directed his word to reveal his will, then he must have spoken in such a way that we would understand.

Genesis tells us that God spoke to the first humans. He selected language as his primary way of communicating with them. Today, God continues to speak with us through his written word. The Apostle Paul assures us that "all Scripture is God-breathed and is useful for teaching, rebuking, correcting and training in righteousness" (2 Timothy 3:16). God's words lay bound between the covers of the Bible. Thus, we can access God's thoughts whenever we open it.

The Power of our Words

In the same way, our words contain amazing power. According to Proverbs a clumsy thrust with our words can injure the people around us, whereas thoughtful advice brings healing and restoration (12:18).

In some cases, our words impart life (Proverbs 18:21a). They can act as a fountain supplying salvation to those who are perishing (1 Corinthians 1:18). In other cases, our words may lead to death (Proverbs 18:21b). Scripture reveals that our words may condemn us on the day of judgment. When God transported Isaiah to his heavenly throne room, Isaiah recoiled at the sight of God's moral perfection. He blurts out the reason he feels alienated from God, "It's all over! I am doomed, for my lips are contaminated by sin." (Isaiah 6:5, NLT). And during his ministry, Jesus announced that God will call us to account for "every careless word" we've spoken (Matthew 12:37). Luckily, believers in Christ will never face God's eternal judgment. But this doesn't minimize the importance of what we say.

God gives us emphatic warnings about how we use our words. Look at how James thunders about the damage our words can cause,

A tiny spark can set a great forest on fire. And among all the parts of the body, the tongue is a flame of fire. It is a whole world of wickedness, corrupting your entire body. It can set your whole life on fire, for it is set on fire by hell itself. People can tame all kinds of animals, birds, reptiles, and fish, but no one can tame the tongue. It is restless and evil, full of deadly poison. Sometimes it praises our Lord and Father, and sometimes it curses those who have been made in the image of God. And so blessing and cursing come pouring out of the same mouth. (James 3:5-10, NLT)

Scripture also teaches that our words expose our true motivations and desires. Whatever spills out of our mouth reveals what sloshes around in our heart. During Jesus' day, most people viewed sin as a virus. They held that you could transmit sin through contact with sinners. But Jesus dismantles this superstitious view of sin with common sense. "Anything you eat passes through the stomach and then goes into the sewer. But the words you speak come from the heart..." (Matthew 15:17-18a, NLT). "For," he explains, "from the heart come evil thoughts, murder, adultery, all sexual immorality, theft, lying, and slander" (Matthew 15:19, NLT).

No wonder, the book of Proverbs devotes more to speech than to any other topic. Since it says so much about the way we use our words, we'll devote two chapters to the impact of our speech. The rest of this chapter will describe words at their worst. The next chapter will discuss words at their best.

Words at Their Worst

We often neglect to see the impact of our words. For instance, some people recklessly fire comments into a crowd with no regard for how their words might injure. Others cause damage with their words in less obvious ways. Like a drone strike, they mar someone's reputation or spark a conflict without leaving a trace.

Brazilian novelist Paul Coelho describes the subtle, yet devastating effect of words:

Of all the weapons of destruction that man could invent, the most terrible –and the most powerful– was the word. Daggers and spears left traces of blood; arrows could be seen at a distance. Poisons were detected in the end and avoided. But the word managed to destroy without leaving clues.[1]

The Apostle Paul includes speech while painting a portrait of human depravity: "Their throats are open graves; their tongues practice deceit. The poison of vipers is on their lips" (Romans 3:13-14). Paul wants us to envision walking toward an open grave and hitting a wall of stench. That's how God feels when he sees us using our words to hurt people or speak against him.

Not to mention, the book of Proverbs describes the damage caused by words at their worst. In particular, it talks about the wreckage left by dishonesty, slander, gossip and outbursts of anger.

Words at their worst *speak dishonestly*

Dishonesty takes many forms. In its most subtle form, it appears as flattery. Flattery describes when you pay someone an insincere compliment. Although it may seem harmless, Proverbs 29:5 warns, "To flatter friends is to lay a net for their feet" (NLT). Often, we use flattery to avoid hurting people's feelings. But a small bruise to their pride may outweigh the long-term injuries sustained from flattery. For example, a parent may use flattery to inflate their child's self-esteem. But that might set their child on a life-course headed toward failure. In its more corrupt form, we use flattery to beguile. We play upon a person's vanity or ego to pry money from their pockets. Or we use insincere compliments to curry favor with people of influence.

Dishonesty also appears in the form of exaggeration. When we recount an outrageous story, we feel tempted to embellish it to get a

---

[1] Paul Coelho, *The Fifth Mountain* (New York: Harper Collins, 2009), 52.

bigger reaction. Or we may adorn a story with details that make us look better.

At other times, dishonesty takes the shape of hypocrisy. Proverbs 26:23-25 denounces someone who feigns spirituality when they've filled their hearts with hate.

Like a coating of glaze over earthenware are fervent lips with an evil heart. The one who hates others disguises it with his lips, but he stores up deceit within him. When he speaks graciously, do not believe him... Though his hatred may be concealed by deceit, his evil will be uncovered in the assembly.

Hypocrisy puts on a false front. It projects an image of self that doesn't fit with reality. This includes hiding sin or concealing a destructive habit.

In its most blatant form, dishonesty appears as a lie. Often, we lie to escape negative consequences. Or we distort the truth to avoid embarrassment. But when the truth exposes us, we face a far worse outcome. Dishonesty hurts our credibility. It damages trust in our relationships and it injures the people to whom we have lied.

In Proverbs 6:16-19, Solomon hands us a list of things God deplores. He starts with six and throws in one more for good measure:

There are six things which the Lord hates, yes, seven which are an abomination to Him: Haughty eyes, a lying tongue, and hands that shed innocent blood, a heart that devises wicked plans, feet that run rapidly to evil, a false witness *who* utters lies, and one who spreads strife among brothers. (Proverbs 6:16-19, NASB)

When you picture an abomination, typically human sacrifice or incest comes to mind. But, you can see why God might view lying as a serious problem. As followers of Christ, God calls on us to proclaim his truth. Truth shields us from the Evil One's fiery accusations. It safeguards us from deception. It transforms our life and liberates people from the bondage of death. That's why uttering lies and skewing the truth grieves God.

Words at their worst *damage people's reputations*

In some cases, we use our words to tarnish someone's reputation. Proverbs 11:9 states, "With their words, the godless destroy their friends, but knowledge will rescue the righteous" (NLT). Our words can alter the way people see someone. Sarcastic remarks, lurid stories and incorrect details leave permanent marks on someone's reputation. And it's hard to repair people's view of someone once they see him/her a certain way.

Several years ago, I organized my home church's annual Thanksgiving dinner. I sent an email to the people in my home church, listing the food items we needed bring. Right away, a woman in our group raised her hand to cook the turkeys. Normally I cook the turkeys, but she seemed eager to do it. So I didn't fight her for it.

As soon as I saw her reply (and I don't know why I did this), I text messaged someone else in our home church, "Sarah said she's going to cook the turkeys. She is probably going to screw them up."

The instant I pressed the send button, I realized I made a terrible mistake. Instead of sending a text message to my friend, I sent it to the woman I was talking about.

I broke into a full body sweat.

Even recalling this incident ties my stomach in knots. I called her right away to apologize. To my surprise, she was very gracious.

Honestly, it's difficult to retrace my steps back to a motive for sending this message. Perhaps I was trying to make my friend laugh. Or maybe I wanted someone to affirm that I could do a better job. Instead of showing gratitude for her willingness to serve, I wanted people to see that she wasn't competent.

Looking back, I'm glad I sent her that message. If I sent it to the other person in my home church, I would've damaged this woman's reputation without a trace. Moreover, God used this shameful experience to impress upon me the damaging effects of words.

Words at their worst *spread gossip*

The New Oxford Dictionary defines gossip as "Casual or unconstrained conversation or reports about other people, typically involving details which are not confirmed as true." Proverbs 18:8 illustrates the deep impression gossip may leave on someone: "The words of a gossip are like choice morsels; they go down to a man's inmost parts." Gossip alters the way we look at people. And once we see someone through a certain lens, it's hard to see him/her differently.

Gossip follows a predictable pattern. People hear a scandalous story. They don't bother to check the facts. They share it with anyone willing to listen like a merchant spreading out his goods on a display table. You won't find a redemptive purpose behind them sharing this story. They're just looking to fill conversation. They share all of the lurid details, placing special emphasis on the worst parts. Perhaps they add their own details to get a bigger response from their listeners.

In its worst form, we employ gossip to alter someone's view of another. In most cases, the helpless victim has no way to mitigate the damage. She's often unaware that people are even talking about her. Derek Kidner depicts the silent damage caused by gossip: "One's attitude to another person may be deeply affected by a mere whisper, unforgettable as soon as relished..."[2]

Gossip erodes trust. Imagine attending a party and your ears perk up because you hear someone talking about *your* personal struggle. You confided in no one else but your friend. You might feel confused, hurt or angry. Either way, you won't make the mistake of telling your friend anything again. Gossips receive the same treatment as mushrooms: you keep them in the dark and feed them a bunch of fertilizer.

Gossip raises suspicion. It destroys relationships and breaks trust. Proverbs 26:20 says, "Without wood a fire goes out; without

---

[2] Kidner, *Proverbs*, 43.

gossip a quarrel dies down." You often find gossips in the eye of a swirling controversy. When they leave, things instantly calm down.

That's one way to tell if you're a gossip. Do quarrels and strife seem to follow you wherever you go? Or ask yourself, "What kind of things do people talk to me about? Do people eagerly bring me fresh gossip?" Proverbs 17:4 says, "Wrongdoers eagerly listen to gossip; liars pay close attention to slander." Chinese Christian author Watchman Nee comments,

> Let us note the kind of talk we enjoy listening to. In this way we can get to know ourselves, for the kind of talk we relish indicates the kind of people we are.

> Some people never confide in you...whereas other people come straight to you and pour into your ears all the latest information they have, because they have sized you up as being the type of person who wants to hear that type of thing. You can judge yourself by stopping to note the things people come and talk to you about.

> As the Lord's servants we come into constant contact with people and have therefore many opportunities of talking and of hearing others talk, so it is essential that we exercise strict control over ourselves lest we become in turn preachers of the Word and relayers of gossip...

> We have to be watchful lest our natural curiosity betray us into hearing more than is good for us to know. There is such a thing as lust for knowledge, lust for information about other people's business, and we must beware of it. We need to be restrained in speech; but if we are to exercise restraint in what we say, then we must first exercise restraint in what we hear.[3]

Now relaying someone's personal information doesn't always fall into the category of gossip. At times, our spouse or friend may confide in us about a complex personal problem. We may feel

---

[3] Watchman Nee, *Normal Christian Worker* (Hong Kong: Hong Kong Church Book Room, 1974), 56.

WORDS AT THEIR WORST

confused or unable to help them. In these cases, we may seek counsel from a wise friend. Conferral doesn't equate to gossip.

But we need to inspect our motives carefully when sharing something a person told us in confidence. Are we looking for advice? Can we share the details of his problem without revealing his identity?

Words at their worst *slander*

Slander is a close relative to gossip. But unlike gossip, slander seeks to misrepresent people and injure their reputation.

In its most passive form, we may jump to conclusions about a story we heard without checking the facts or seeking the other side of the story. Or we attach a sinister motive to something a person said. Then we broadcast what we've heard after adding our spin. Those listening greedily devour it and share it with others. Like an infestation overrunning a house, the story spreads.

Once the helpless victim discovers what people have been saying about her, slander has left its mark. Like finding a single termite in the floorboards of a house, there's no way for the victim to determine how much damage their reputation sustained.

In other cases, we can raise suspicion through subtle comments or even signaling with our body. We can introduce doubt by raising an eyebrow or shooting a smirk at someone across the room. Proverbs lists the various kinds of "sinister sign language" we use to insinuate.[4] "A worthless and wicked person walks around saying perverse things; he winks with his eyes, signals with his feet, and points with his fingers; he plots evil with perverse thoughts in his heart, he spreads contention at all times" (Proverbs 6:12-14, NET).

Beyond damaging a person's reputation, slander can rip apart entire spiritual communities. The wise man warns, "A wicked scoundrel digs up evil, and his slander is like a scorching fire. A perverse person spreads dissension" (Proverbs 16:27-28, NET). Several years ago, I visited one of the largest churches in America.

---

[4] The NET Bible note on Proverbs 6:12-14.

67

When I walked into their new stadium-style auditorium, two-thirds of the seats were empty. After the service, I turned to the woman sitting next to me and asked why the crowd at their main service looked thin. I discovered that they went through a nasty division, which ravaged their church. It resulted in a mass exodus of more than half its members.

I've seen the same thing happen on a smaller scale. A number of years ago, a guy attending one of our home churches grew angry because people confronted him about abusing alcohol. His anger morphed into bitterness and he started planting seeds of dissension in his group. He claimed that "getting drunk isn't a big deal because we're all under grace." He suggested the Bible teaches a more "radical" form of grace than we taught. On his way out the door, he convinced several others to leave.

Words at their worst *speak in anger*

Words spoken in anger always end in regret. "An angry man stirs up dissension, and a hot-tempered one commits many sins" (Proverbs 29:22). Giving vent to our anger may be one of the most satisfying *and* damaging ways to use our speech. Angry exchanges shatter families and leave lasting scars on our friendships.

Speaking in anger nearly cost me my ministry. I grew up in a home where it was normal to lash out in anger. At that time, psychologists encouraged people to "let out" their anger. They compared anger to a pressure cooker. You need to vent your anger; otherwise you might explode. But recent studies show that unleashing your anger doesn't make you less angry. It leads to further aggression. According to the American Psychological Association, 'Research has found that "letting it rip" with anger actually escalates anger and aggression and does nothing to help you.'[5]

As a result, I would lash out at people whenever I felt like they were ganging up on me or disrespecting me. Or I would say the

---

[5] "Controlling anger before it controls you," American Psychological Association," http://www.apa.org/topics/anger/control.aspx

cruelest thing that came to mind. During the awkward silence following an angry outburst, I would say to myself, "That's right. That'll teach them to mess with me like that." It felt good to silence them. At the time, I didn't account for the long-term damage these outbursts might cause to my friendships or to my credibility as God's spokesman.

But God used an incident with one of my roommates to show me the gravity of losing my temper. Shortly after I started leading for God, I got into an argument with my roommate. The argument escalated and I started shouting and cursing at him. News of the incident quickly reached my spiritual mentor. That week, I met with him and he asked me what happened. After I confessed what had happened, he gently explained, "When you fly off the handle and say something in anger, you can't take it back. That person may forgive you, but they'll have a hard time looking at you the same way." When you unleash your fury on someone or say something cruel, it makes that person reluctant to draw close to you. That person might start tiptoeing around you. She may even comply with things you tell her to do, just to avoid getting sprayed by a verbal eruption. But you've lost her respect. Fear works when you want to intimidate people, but it's bad for building close relationships.

In other cases, speaking in anger takes the form of passive aggression. Maybe our home didn't resemble a battlefield whenever conflict arose. Perhaps it resembled a cold war. Bitterness and resentment chilled the relationships within our family. At times, the building friction would surface in subtle jabs or mean spirited comments. Maybe we watched as our family took aim at each other with surgical precision. Years later, we can still quote hurtful comments verbatim. It's as if we've been rehearsing that event over and over again in our mind.

Taming the Tongue

Many of us find ourselves guilty of doing one or more of the above. Perhaps, some of us never received guidance about our speech. No one sat us down and explained the damaging effects of gossip and slander, which were fixtures of our home growing up. As a result, we view them as topics that naturally appear in the course of a conversation. Maybe we grew up in an environment where it was common to lash out in anger or we even had a Christian mentor whose gossip or slander went unchecked by others. Now we find ourselves doing the same thing to our spouse, children and close friends.

Maybe you've felt a growing conviction that God desires to see you change in the area of your speech. Maybe you're currently embroiled in conflict because of a careless exchange with a friend. Or maybe you're trying to repair a damaged friendship because of a caustic remark you've made. It's important for you to see that any self-improvement project aimed at changing your speech will fail.

According to Jesus, God must transform our hearts in order to transform our words. In Matthew 15:18-19, Jesus states, "The words you speak come from the heart...For from the heart come evil thoughts..." (NLT). That's why Paul urges us, "Don't copy the behavior and customs of this world, but let God transform you into a new person by changing the way you think" (Romans 12:1, NLT). If we're striving to see real change, we need more than restraint of speech. We must permit God to transform the thoughts from which our words spring.

Furthermore, our membership in God's spiritual community should challenge the way we speak to one another. Rather than tearing each other down, God calls us to build each other up. We need to offer more than just resistance if we plan to see victory over gossip, slander and speaking in anger. We must replace these with positive speech (Ephesians 4:31-32). Maybe the next time we feel an impulse to slander someone, we should try praising that person for a strength they possess. Or if we sense ourselves about to gossip, we should substitute it with a story aimed at building up someone's reputation (1 Corinthians 14:26).

For Further Discussion:

1. Why do we often fail to see the impact of our words?

2. Do you find yourself falling into any of these negative patterns of speech? If so, which one?
3. How have you seen negative speech impact your relationships?

WORDS AT THEIR BEST

Never underestimate the power of your words. Jean-Paul Sartre once said, "Words are loaded pistols." Our words contain the power to either take a life or impart life. That's why Proverbs gives us this solemn reminder: "Death and life are in the power of the tongue" (Proverbs 18:21).

In the previous chapter, we mainly looked at the damaging effects of our words. In this chapter, we will examine how we can use our words to transform lives.

Words at their best *impart spiritual life and healing*

We live in a profoundly broken world, filled with broken people. We yearn for a solution to our problems, turning to self-help seminars, treatment facilities and antidepressants. Yet, inner turmoil remains a fixture in our lives. Like driving with a missing side mirror, we find ways to live with our struggles. Or we turn to destructive habits to manage our depression and anxiety.

Where can we turn to gain freedom? According to Jesus, God's truth contains the power to liberate us from false beliefs and destructive patterns that keep us in bondage (John 8:32). Thus, wielding Scripture holds the power to transform people's lives.

The world's wisdom lacks transforming power because it traces its origin back to human speculation, whereas Scripture claims to impart God's revelation. The author of Hebrews portrays the word of God as "living and active and sharper than any double-edged sword, piercing even to the point of dividing soul from spirit, and joints from marrow; it is able to judge the desires and thoughts of the heart" (4:12, NASB). Scripture doesn't represent ancient man's explanation for the world before the advent of modern science. God's written word transcends time and culture, since God stands outside both.

That's why I make sure to use Scripture whenever I give people counsel. I want to make it clear I'm not just giving them my opinion

73

or communicating my expectations. Rather, I'm directing them toward what God says. Failing to guide people to God's word can obscure what we're trying to communicate. They may leave the conversation with the impression that we're placing heavy demands on them or that the problem lies between them and us. If we don't anchor our counsel in accurate application of God's truth, we risk manipulating others with our personal desires. As the author of Hebrews pointed out, God's word has the power to convict and direct on its own. Therefore, we gain confidence to speak truth when we bring God's word into the center of a difficult conversation. It relieves the pressure we feel to change people and relies on God's power to accomplish the change.

In our fellowship, it's common to hear people describe how God spoke to them through other believers. Recently, I heard a story about how God spoke to a woman who attended one of our leadership gatherings. At one point, she described feeling as if the whole room dimmed and someone shined a spotlight on her. The person speaking said something that was already rattling around in her mind. She felt as if God was speaking directly to her in that moment.

God speaks through people like this all the time. In fact, he insists on using human agency as his primary method of speaking to the world. Thus, God may be waiting on us to speak for him and our reluctance to study Scripture or to open our mouths might impede him from using us.

Words at their best *revive those feeling discouraged*

In other cases, our words may revive a believer on the verge of abandoning the race. Our words may give this brother or sister in Christ renewed strength, like a runner who grimaces with determination as she passes a family member who's shouting, "Keep going!"

After my first year following God, I went through a crisis. My feelings of excitement for God were starting to disappear. Doubts began to appear in my mind. During one of our large meetings, I left in the middle of the teaching to get some air. A woman from my home church was standing outside. She asked, "What's wrong?" I explained how my excitement for God was waning. After asking a few questions, she said, "I wonder if God may be switching gears with you. It seems like he wants you to move from demanding that people love and serve you, to loving and serving others." As soon as she said that, it clicked in my head. She put into words what I was wrestling with at that moment. I walked back inside with a renewed sense of vision and excitement. That conversation took place in 10 minutes. Seventeen years later, I still view it as a pivotal event in my walk with God.

Words at their best *rescue those who are perishing*

Solomon gives us the sober reminder that "Death and life are in the power of the tongue" (Proverbs 18:21, NET). He also says, "A truthful witness saves lives, but he who utters lies is treacherous" (Proverbs 14:25, NASB). In the context, Solomon was talking about a witness testifying in a court of law. In Israel, you could convict someone based on the testimony of two or three witnesses. But this proverb takes on a whole new meaning when we turn to the pages of New Testament.

The Bible maintains that our moral-wrongdoing alienates us from God. And our alienation will someday lead to eternal separation from him. Luckily, God sent his son Jesus to pay for our sins. The Bible declares that we can only experience forgiveness through Jesus' payment on the cross. We cannot earn right-standing before God; we must receive it.

Now if Jesus came to die for our sins, then the Good News about his death becomes one of the most important things we can tell people. The message of Christ can rescue those who are perishing. Proverbs 24:11-12 provides this exhortation:

Rescue those being led away to death; hold back those staggering toward slaughter. If you say, 'But we knew nothing about this,' does not he who weighs the heart perceive it? Does not he who guards your life know it? Will he not repay each person according to what he has done? (NET)

How would you view someone if he failed to testify and it led to a wrongful conviction? Or what would you say if it resulted in someone's execution? It would probably spark moral outrage in you. Wouldn't it be even more grievous if someone's testimony could prevent someone's eternal death and yet he refused to speak up?

That's why Jesus commissions us to carry out his mission. He says, "You will be my witnesses in Jerusalem, and in all Judea and Samaria, and to the ends of the earth" (Acts 1:8). Jesus handed his disciples the baton right before he ascended to heaven. He charged his followers to act as witnesses to what they saw and heard. He called on them to go to the remote parts of the earth to testify about the Good News of his death.

Most people in our culture show resistance to Christianity. If you introduce Christianity to a discussion, people's minds don't gravitate toward God's love or the Good News. Most people associate the Bible with bad news that we need to do good things and avoid bad things to escape God's judgment. So we need to speak with wisdom, seeking to dismantle people's faulty views about God and the Bible. Further, we should seek to use our words to lovingly and sensitively stimulate spiritual thoughts or persuade people to turn to Christ.

Words at their best *restore those enslaved to sin*

Sin dims our spiritual outlook. People entangled in sin often convince themselves that only sin can make them happy. They surrender small amounts of freedom as they yield themselves to sin –until they find themselves completely enslaved to it.

In other cases, people feel trapped by sin. They feel as if they'll never change. Over the years, I've talked to countless people who've said, "I just can't help it. I've tried to stop, but I can't." And when I explain that we're no longer slaves to sin (Romans 6:6-7), they look amazed. God's truth awakens them to the false beliefs holding them captive.

God brings loving correction into our lives because he loves us (Hebrews 12:6). Stated negatively: if God doesn't correct us, it suggests we aren't his children (Hebrews 12:8). Solomon urges us to see the big picture while enduring God's discipline when he says "My child, don't reject the Lord's discipline, and don't be upset when he corrects you. For the Lord corrects those he loves, just as a father corrects a child in whom he delights" (Proverbs 3:11-12, NLT).

Hearing the truth may sting. But when someone speaks with a spirit of gentleness and love, their words can convey God's love in ways that very few things can.

Words at their best *come from careful listening*

Listening isn't as easy as it might seem. For example, people will call attention to someone else's part in a conflict while excluding details about their own. A good listener will quickly detect the missing information. "Wait, so you didn't do anything, and she just started shouting at you?" Or when someone gives a partial confession, the listener might ask, "What exactly do you mean by, 'It's been a while'?" A trained ear can discern when the story doesn't add up.

At times people will come to us in a confused state asking us for counsel. They can describe how they feel, but they can't put their finger on the problem. Like a doctor, we must provide an accurate diagnosis of their spiritual condition as we listen to them describe their symptoms. Unlike a physician, we don't have access to other diagnostic tools. We possess only one: our ears.

If we're unable to give people a careful hearing, we'll never arrive at their true spiritual condition. Moreover, our advice will miss the mark. Bad listeners will hear something and instantly attach their subjective impression to what they hear. Often they conclude something that was never in the mind of the speaker. By contrast, good listeners allow what they hear to challenge their assumptions. They listen before arriving at a conclusion. Good listeners can discern the meaning of both what a person says and what he's failing to say.

Bad listeners act as if they already know what you will say before you say it. Proverbs 18:13 says, "Spouting off before listening to the facts is both shameful and foolish" (NLT). In some cases, poor listeners will interrupt you mid-sentence and try to finish your thought. But they're completely wrong! We glare at them, wait for them to stop sucking up all the oxygen in the room and then finish what we were going to say.

What a difference it makes when you explain a problem to someone who actually listens. You walk away feeling understood. And that person usually gives you helpful advice.[1]

Words at their best *speak honestly*

Proverbs 24:26 says, "An honest answer is like a kiss on the lips." I guess that's a good thing, depending on who it's from. Spiritual battles have been lost and won on the ground of God's truth. Truth releases people from bondage and imparts spiritual life. But our ability to convey truth relates to our credibility as speakers. Withheld details, embellished stories and outright lies damage our credibility.

Often we lie because we feel embarrassed or ashamed about something we've done. But lying only compounds the problem. Concealing the truth requires a lot of energy. We must fabricate new lies to cover up old ones. Our heads spin when we try to keep different versions of our stories organized in our minds. At times, we can't even recall whom we told which lie. And when the truth finally comes out, it unravels our web of lies and we find ourselves facing serious and difficult consequences.

Some of us never learned the value of telling the truth. We've gotten into the habit of lying to get out of a jam. For some of us, the habit of lying has hardened into a character flaw. At times, we catch ourselves lying and we can't even explain why we're doing it.

If we want to break this pattern of compulsive lying, we must force ourselves to go back to people when we realize we've lied to them. In many cases, we'll feel silly for lying when we see their reaction to the truth. We should also authorize spiritual friends to

---

[1] Nee, *Normal Christian Worker*, 41-50.

question us if something we say raises an eyebrow. Over time, we will see that admitting the truth isn't that bad. More importantly, we will experience God's grace when we confess (James 5:16).

On the other hand, I've met people who swing to the opposite extreme. They feel as if they must tell people every thought that enters their minds. But we need to balance honesty with discretion. Solomon gives us this humorous simile, "Like a gold ring in a pig's snout [so] is a beautiful woman who shows no discretion" (Proverbs 11:22). Discretion refers to the quality of speaking with care. It describes the ability to restrain ourselves from saying too much.

Wisdom suggests that honesty is actually *not* always the best policy. Discretion keeps our close relationships intact. Imagine losing the ability to filter your thoughts. Whatever pops into your head dribbles out of your mouth. What would your relationships look like? Your wife walks up to you and asks, "Do I look fat in this dress?" "Absolutely," you say without hesitation.

In other cases, the inability to filter words can cause permanent damage. It's neither helpful nor redemptive when a husband tells his wife in the heat of an argument, "I wonder if I made a mistake marrying you." Even if he and his wife work out their marital problems, he can never take back his words. They remain etched in her memory. And they may resurface in (and fuel) future arguments. So before you share something, make a habit of asking yourself: Will I regret saying this later? Is there redemptive value in what I'm planning on saying? Asking yourself these questions will save you a lot of trouble and embarrassment. Take it from someone who has gotten himself into a lot of trouble because of careless words. Or take it from someone wise like Solomon, who said, "An evil man is trapped by his sinful talk, but a righteous man escapes trouble" (Proverbs 12:13).

Words at their best *will be few*

Fools can disguise themselves with silence. The wise man observes, "Even a fool, when he keeps silent, is considered wise; when he closes his lips, he is *considered* prudent" (Proverbs 17:28, NASB).

Envision a fool talking to someone. At times, he peers into the sky with a look of concentration on his face. At points, he nods his head while squinting his eyes. You might conclude, "This guy seems wise." But then he blows his cover as soon as he opens his mouth.

Most of the time, we get in trouble because we can't keep our mouths shut. Proverbs 21:23 says, "Watch your tongue and keep your mouth shut, and you will stay out of trouble." In another place, the wise man remarks, "When words are many, sin is not absent, but he who holds his tongue is wise' (Proverbs 10:19). Most extreme talkers have never encountered someone who explained to them that talkers appear foolish. At most, people just made fun of them. Even when they're saying something insightful, people often dismiss them, concluding that they're saying something stupid.

One of the guys I used to mentor talked nonstop. His philosophy in life was simple: When in doubt, speak. He possessed an uncanny ability to extract sensitive information from people in a conversation. But he didn't pry it from them by asking good questions. People would tell him whatever he wanted to know, just to get him to stop talking. Finally, I sat him down and explained that effective Christian workers learn to use an economy of words. Words are like cologne: less is more.

Jesus showed us the power of silence. His silence was deafening as he stood before the Jewish rulers and Pilate. J. Oswald Sanders muses on Jesus' silence,

> It is always more difficult to remain silent than to speak. But on three occasions it is recorded of the Lord that He was silent before His enemies... In each case His silence was immeasurably more eloquent than any spoken word could possibly have been.[2]

---

[2] J. Oswald Sanders, *The Incomparable Christ* (Chicago: Moody Classics, 2009), 218.

Words at their best *are well-timed*

Proverbs 25:11 paints this word picture: "*Like* apples of gold in settings of silver is a word spoken in right circumstances" (NASB). The wise man highlights how the timing and content of our words complement each other. If we were to use a modern simile, it would sound like this: "Like a perfectly paired wine with a great meal, so are words spoken at just the right time." The right words spoken at the right time contain great value.

According to modern psychology, the timing of words can determine their level of impact. For example, if you encourage your daughter right after she does something right, it makes a bigger impact than telling her the same thing two weeks later.

In some cases, well-timed words can alter someone's life. Fifteen years ago, I shared during my baptism how I met Christ. Right after I finished talking, a guy walked up to me and said, "Did you notice that people were captivated while you were sharing your story? I wonder if God has given you a speaking gift." Up to that point, the thought of speaking for God never entered my mind. But that conversation planted a seed. From that moment, I quietly started taking steps toward becoming a Bible teacher. His words rerouted the destination of my life. I'm sure he never envisioned the impact his words would have on me.

Timing also plays an important role when we provide loving correction. Postponing a difficult conversation usually creates more problems than it solves. Avoiding a hard conversation gives people more time to redact their narrative. Excuses, selective memory and a creative recollection paint them in a better light. Or if we wait too long to address an issue, the person may feel blindsided. They might claim, "That happened a month ago. Why are we talking about it now? I've made progress since then."

So what holds us back from speaking words of loving correction? Usually it's fear. We dread the awkward feeling of raising a concern. We fear that the person may get angry, or worse, that he might reject us. But if our love for that person outweighs the personal cost we might pay, speaking the truth will override our fears.

Words at their best *are thoughtful*

It's not just what we say that's important; it's how we say it. "The heart of the righteous weighs its answers, but the mouth of the wicked gushes evil" (Proverb 15:28). The wise person carefully weighs how his words will impact people. Whenever I enter an important conversation, I try to visualize how the person may respond to things I say. Preparing for their reaction helps me to avoid feeling caught off guard.

This process carries even more importance for reflective thinkers. Reflective thinkers require time to process information. They gain insight by carefully tumbling things over in their mind. If someone slaps them with something they've never heard, they get confused and don't know what to say. For those of us with this tendency, we must spend even more time preparing for important talks.

You can tell when thoughtful friends have spent time mulling over your situation. They can describe your thoughts and doubts. They don't supply you with stock answers; rather, they've tailored their advice to your situation. It appears as if they've placed themselves in your shoes. This makes us more willing to listen. And we walk away from such conversations feeling loved.

On the part of the speaker, speaking for God provides us with deep fulfillment. "A man finds joy in giving an apt reply – and how good is a timely word!" (Proverbs 15:23). There's nothing quite like the feeling of God speaking through you. You sense God's spirit directing your words as they come out of your mouth. You hear yourself saying things you would *never* have come up with, even if you spent several hours planning what to say. You can see that the person listening resonates with what you're saying. The exhilaration you feel when God works through you brings a sense of fulfillment unlike anything else.

Heightening the Impact of Our Words

Solomon says, "For the LORD gives wisdom; from His mouth come knowledge and understanding" (Proverbs 2:6). All wisdom traces back to God as its source. God promises he will lavish wisdom upon us if we ask for it (James 1:5). He also makes his wisdom available through the Scriptures. God reveals who he is and what he has done for us through his written word. Absorbing God's word and letting it saturate our thinking will increase the impact of our words.

Allowing God to change our character will also heighten the impact of our words. God cares as much about the person speaking as he does about the words spoken. The wise person observes, "The heart of the wise instructs his mouth and adds persuasiveness to his lips" (Proverbs 16:23, NET). What you say relates to who you are. Jesus put this differently when he said, "For out of the overflow of the heart the mouth speaks" (Matthew 12:34). What comes *out* of your mouth speaks volumes about what's *in* your heart. Thus, the quality and impact of your words increase in proportion to the change God has brought about in your character.

For Further Discussion:

1. Our ability to impact people with our words relates to our ability to listen. What are some ways you can improve as a listener?
2. Why is it difficult to convey the truth accurately?
3. Share a personal experience where God used someone to speak truth in your life.

THE DANGERS OF WEALTH

This doesn't exactly have the ring of a popular sermon title. But it's what we need to hear. For more than half a century, the American church has consorted with the enemy. We've perfected a dicey balance between frenzied materialism and lukewarm spirituality.

Proverbs speaks to the topic of wealth, listing the dangers of possessing too much money and too many possessions. Let's briefly survey this list.

Wealth slowly numbs us to our need for God

In Proverbs 30:7-9, the wise man appeals to God:

> O God, I beg two favors from you; let me have them before I die. First, help me never to tell a lie. Second, give me neither poverty nor riches! Give me just enough to satisfy my needs. For if I grow rich, I may deny you and say, "Who is the Lord?" And if I am too poor, I may steal and thus insult God's holy name. (NLT)

When most of us pray, we ask God to deliver us from poverty. But the thought probably never enters our mind to ask him to rescue us from wealth.

Wealth leaves us feeling self-satisfied. Most of us never say to ourselves, "How am I going to eat?" or "Where will I get my next meal?" Most of the time, we ask ourselves, "What do I feel like eating?" or "Should I keep eating?" When Jesus provided us an example of how to pray, he included, "Give us this day our daily bread." He was showing us that we should depend on God for our needs. But what's the point of praying for daily bread when you happen to own a bakery?

It's easy to ignore God when you live in abundance. In Revelation 3:15-17, Jesus sharply rebukes the Laodicean church:

> I know your deeds, that you are neither cold nor hot. I wish you were either one or the other! So, because you are lukewarm — neither hot nor cold — I am about to spit you out of my mouth.

You say, "I am rich; I have acquired wealth and do not need a thing." But you do not realize that you are wretched, pitiful, poor, blind and naked.

Materialism blinds us from seeing our spiritual need. It dims our spiritual perception. It reduces our gnawing spiritual hunger into a rumble we can ignore. John Steinbeck once wrote,

> A strange species we are...We can stand anything God and nature can throw at us save only plenty. If I wanted to destroy a nation, I would give it too much, and I would have it on its knees, miserable, greedy, sick.[1]

Having more doesn't quench our materialistic thirst

We get a brief surge of excitement when we tear open the package containing our new device. Or a wave of euphoria hits us when we hand a sales associate our credit card to purchase a new pair of shoes. Yet, these feelings quickly evaporate. We long to experience that rush again. So we buy even more.

But over time, nothing we purchase can mask the emptiness we feel. Money and possessions will never leave us feeling full because we're trying to fill what Blaise Pascal called the "infinite abyss." God designed us to be in a relationship with him. Only he can satisfy what's missing.

Yet, we find ourselves unable to disrupt this cycle of materialism. We can't control our impulse to spend. We feel trapped in a rat race of career advancement. We're unable to turn down opportunities to make more money, even if it impacts our family and friendships.

In many ways, materialism resembles some of the worst addictions that afflict our culture. You could easily replace "alcoholism" or "prescription pill addiction" with materialism. Yet, most people don't view materialism as harmful. In fact, our culture guides people toward a materialistic way of life.

---

[1] John Steinbeck, quoted in Richard Halverson, *Perspective*, June 24, 1987.

Many of us grew up with parents who were hopelessly addicted to materialism. They bought us all the stuff we wanted. But they never gave us the one thing we wanted most: time with them. Sadly, we're likely to repeat this pattern unless we turn to God for help.

Wealth threatens to highjack the security we place in Christ

Proverbs 18:11 observes, "A rich man's wealth is his strong city, and like a high wall in his own imagination" (NASB). Some of us criticize people who flash their wealth. We consider it tacky when someone vaunts her designer clothes or expensive jewelry. Or we sneer when she pulls up in a brand new sports car.

We feel more drawn to gaining financial security. We store up our wealth in stocks, retirement funds and savings accounts. Viewing our monthly statement or online account brings us a sense of security. But the Proverbs warn, "He who trusts in his riches will fall, but the righteous will flourish like the green leaf" (Proverbs 11:28, NASB). As Christians, we don't believe in financial security – we believe in eternal security.

A few years ago, my friend's dad passed away. He suffered a massive heart attack and died instantly. When my friend was sharing how his dad's death affected him, he noted, "My dad was obsessed with retiring. He funneled most of his time and energy into making sure he had a cushy retirement. Any time I spent with him, he would talk about it." Then my friend paused and said, "It's sad because he never saw a day of retirement. He died just days before." When we strive to attain financial security, we're investing in something with no ultimate future.

Having too much can create anxiety

Proverbs 15:16 says, "Better a little with the fear of the LORD than great wealth with turmoil." In his famous Sermon on the Mount, Jesus drew a straight line connecting anxiety and materialism. He concludes his lengthy critique of materialism with these words:

So don't worry about these things, saying, "What will we eat? What will we drink? What will we wear?" These things dominate the thoughts of unbelievers, but your heavenly Father already knows all your needs. Seek the Kingdom of God above all else, and live righteously, and he will give you everything you need. (Matthew 6:31-33)

The things we own may eventually own us. The more things we own, the more we have to worry about. I remember when my wife and I lived in a tiny one-bedroom apartment. When something broke, we didn't fix it. We called our landlord and *he* fixed it. I found little to complain about in our little apartment, except that the Asian restaurant next door aimed its exhaust fan at our apartment. When we opened our windows during the summer, our place would smell like Mongolian beef.

Now we own a house. That places the responsibility to maintain and repair it on our shoulders. If my furnace takes its last breath, the money comes out of my pocket to fix it. If my lawn starts looking like a wild prairie, I'm responsible to mow it. We didn't deal with any of these headaches when we lived in our one-bedroom apartment.

You could say the same thing for other purchases. When you trade in your 15-year-old car for an expensive new car, all of a sudden you're paranoid that someone might dent it. If you purchase a new couch, you feel on edge when people put their feet on it. Or you may feel reluctant to host gatherings at your house because you don't want people to track dirt onto your new white carpet.

It takes time and energy to maintain your possessions. And you must reclaim that time and energy from somewhere else. When you fuss and tinker with the classic car you plan to restore, that's time you could spend with your family. When you spend several hours setting up your new high definition TV and surround sound, you could spend that time cultivating intimacy with God. Randy Alcorn offers a grim prognosis for anyone who allows their possessions to overrun their lives:

> What will happen to the affluent person or society that does not rectify its materialism? The basic laws of physics give us the

answer. The greater the mass, the greater the hold that mass exerts. This explains why the largest planets are capable of holding so many satellites in orbit. Similarly, the more things we own—the greater their total mass—the more they grip us, hold us, set us in orbit around them. Finally, like a black hole, a gargantuan cosmic vacuum cleaner, they mercilessly suck us into themselves, until we become indistinguishable from our things, surrendering ourselves to the inhuman gods we have idolized.[2]

Our wealth can't purchase for us what we need most

Proverbs 11:4 observes, "Wealth is worthless in the day of wrath, but righteousness delivers from death" The Bible declares that we will all stand before God at the end of our lives. All of our money and possessions will lose their value on that day. None of it will help redeem us. The psalmist states it forcefully:

> Why should I fear when trouble comes, when enemies surround me? They trust in their wealth and boast of great riches. Yet, they cannot redeem themselves from death by paying a ransom to God. Redemption does not come so easily, for no one can ever pay enough to live forever and never see the grave. (Psalm 49:5-9, NLT)

Alcorn has thoughts on this as well:

> The only thing worth buying cannot be bought with money. God's Son bought us our salvation, and freely gives himself to all who seek him. Money cannot buy salvation, and it cannot buy rescue from judgment.[3]

Materialism may lead to partiality and mistreatment of the poor.

Proverbs 19:7 tells us, "All the brothers of a poor man hate him; how much more do his friends abandon him! He pursues *them with*

---

[2] Randy Alcorn, *Money, Possessions, and Eternity* (Carol Stream, IL: Tyndale House Publishers, 2003), 35.

[3] Ibid., 50.

words, *but* they are gone" (NASB). By contrast, people highly esteem the rich and famous. They gravitate toward the rich because the rich possess what their eyes lust after. People fawn over the rich and try to impress their friends –casually mentioning with whom they spent the weekend. Or they hope that groveling to the rich will open new opportunities. Yet, they ignore those whom they consider "have-nots."

In some cases, materialism leads to oppression of the poor. Scripture reveals that God fiercely defends the rights of the poor. Or to state it in the negative: God abhors when the rich exploit the poor. Let me give you a small sample of what God says to the rich in Proverbs:

> He who oppresses the poor shows contempt for their Maker, but whoever is kind to the needy honors God. (14:31)
>
> A poor man's field may produce abundant food, but injustice sweeps it away. (13:23)
>
> A poor man pleads for mercy, but a rich man answers harshly. (18:23)
>
> Wealth brings many friends, but a poor man's friend deserts him. (19:4)
>
> A poor man is shunned by all his relatives –how much more do his friends avoid him! Though he pursues them with pleading, they are nowhere to be found. (19:7)
>
> The rich rule over the poor, and the borrower is servant to the lender. (22:7)
>
> He who oppresses the poor to increase his wealth and he who gives gifts to the rich—both come to poverty. (22:16)
>
> Do not exploit the poor because they are poor and do not crush the needy in court, for the Lord will take up their case and will plunder those who plunder them. (22:22-23)
>
> Do not move an ancient boundary stone or encroach on the fields of the fatherless, for their Defender is strong; he will take up their case against you. (23:10-11)

However, it's not enough to avoid exploiting the poor; God tells us we shouldn't turn away when we see their plight. According to the Proverbs:

> If a man shuts his ears to the cry of the poor, he too will cry out and not be answered. (21:13)

> The righteous care about justice for the poor, but the wicked have no such concern. (29:7)

Who are the wicked in these proverbs? They're people who aren't "concerned for the rights of the poor." They change the channel when images of grinding poverty flash on the screen. After all, they wouldn't want these unsavory images to ruin their nice dinner. But God calls on his followers to show compassion to the poor.

And God calls for more than just compassion. He challenges us to open our hearts *and* our wallets to the poor. Proverbs 19:17 says, "He who is kind to the poor lends to the LORD, and he will reward him for what he has done." This mirrors what Jesus told his disciples in Matthew 25, "For I was hungry and you gave me something to eat, I was thirsty and you gave me something to drink" (v35). His followers asked him, "When did we do these things?" Jesus replied, "Whatever you did for one of the least of these brothers of mine, you did for me" (25:39). According to these passages, the way we view the poor reflects the way we view God.

Not to mention, if we invest in things containing spiritual value, we'll see a return on our investment. Jesus promises that if we sacrifice for the sake of the poor in this life, God will give us 100 times as much in the next. So we shouldn't view what we give as a sacrifice; we should view it as investment into the future. Never worry about outgiving God.

Relative Wealth

Some of you might say, "I'm not rich." You might point to a millionaire and say, "They're rich. I'm just barely making it." Most of us represent the middle class. Some of us even fall below the median income. Still others would say, "I'm a poor college student. I eat packages of ramen noodles for dinner."

But would it be accurate for us to say, "I'm just barely making it?" Perhaps our surroundings distort our perception of wealth. If we compare our income to the rest of the world, things look a little different.

In 2013, the U.S. Census Bureau reported the median household income was $51,939. If your household income lands at or above this figure, you fall into the category of wealthiest 1% of the world.

Even the most impoverished in America still rank among the wealthiest in the world. In America, a family of four stands right on the poverty line at $23,850. Yet, they still fall within the top 3% compared to the rest of the world. It's hard to envision this if you've never traveled to developing nations and seen how the rest of the world lives.

Economist Jeffrey Sachs claims the international poverty line stands at around $1 a day. In October 2015, World Bank released an updated figure of $1.90 a day. Now this figure factors in what they call purchasing-power parity –where you adjust income for equivalent purchasing power. In other words, it accounts for how a dollar would spend in both the United States and Costa Rica for the same pound of rice.

Several years ago, I taught a leadership seminar in Cambodia. During one of our breaks, I asked my translator, "How much does an average Cambodian earn in a day?" He said, "Before translating, I was making about $1 a day, doing construction." Keep in mind: this doesn't include health insurance or other benefits. He was making $10 a day as a translator, which catapulted him into the category of a "wealthy" Cambodian.

Several years ago, *The Economist* ran an article called "The Mountain Man and the Surgeon." It compared the lives of an unemployed coal miner from Eastern Kentucky and a prominent doctor from the Democratic Republic of Congo.

Enos Banks lives in a trailer nestled in the hills of the Appalachian Mountains. Half a dozen stripped and rusted cars adorn his front yard. Mr. Banks collects $521 a month in

Supplemental Security Income (SSI), which the US government provides for elderly, disabled and low-income households.

Thousands of miles away, Dr. Kabamba heads the emergency department at Kinshasa General Hospital, located in the Congolese capital. After 28 years of practicing medicine, Dr. Kabamba earns $250 a month. He earns an additional $400 a month operating a private practice after hours. The author of the article, Joy Fauntleroy, draws a comparison between these men:

> Given the lower cost of living in Congo, one might guess that Dr. Kabamba is better off than Mr. Banks. But the doctor has to support an extended family of 12, whereas Mr. Banks's ex-wife and three sons claim public assistance. Indeed, the reason Mr. Banks split up from his wife, he says, is because they can draw more benefits separately. She still lives in the trailer next door.[4]

Dr. Kabamba's income affords him a four-bedroom house with a kitchen and a living room. Not bad, even by American standards. But it feels a little cramped with the 12 people living there. To offer a point of comparison, only 6% of American households live in a home with more occupants than rooms.

In America, most poor households have two TVs and cable or satellite service. And nearly three quarters of poor households enjoy air-conditioning. By contrast, Dr. Kabamba's family lacks running water. They fetch their water in jars, daily. And electricity comes on twice a week, if they're lucky.

To highlight the gap between the wealthiest of an impoverished country and the poorest of a wealthy country, we should look at what their income buys them to eat.

Dr. Kabamba earns enough to feed his children, but not as well as he would like. The family eats meat about twice a month; Dr. Kabamba calls it "a great luxury". In America, poor children eat more meat than the well-to-do. In fact, they get twice as much

---

[4] The Economist, "The Mountain Man and the Surgeon: Reflections on relative poverty in North America and Africa," last modified December 20, 2005, http://www.economist.com/node/5323888

protein as their government says is good for them, which is why the Wal-Mart near Mr. Banks sells such enormous jeans…All one can say is that whereas the poor in Kinshasa complain about the price of bread, the poor in Kentucky complain about the price of motor insurance.[5]

Now I'm not trying to belittle America's poor. Nor am I trying to make light of the struggles they face. I'm simply trying to place our view of wealth into a larger context. Fauntleroy summarizes, "A Congolese doctor, a man most other Congolese would consider wealthy, is worse off materially than most poor people in America." To put it differently, the rest of the world would view an unemployed coal miner from Eastern Kentucky as "wealthy." The 2.8 billion people in the world –living on less than $2 a day– would gladly trade places with the 47 million Americans living below the poverty line.

While wealth increases your risk of materialism, poverty doesn't immunize you from it. Several years ago, our church sent a team to Cambodia for a short-term mission trip. During the trip, our partner organization's country director asked our team to share a few thoughts with her national workers. Specifically, she asked them to describe some of the challenges they face in ministry. Some people on the team explained that wealth blocks people in our culture from seeing their spiritual need. Those who shared felt uneasy about telling people with very little that they suffer from having too much.

Afterward, the country director bounded toward the team and exclaimed, "That's exactly what our leaders needed to hear!" One of the team members looked at her with his forehead crinkled. He broke into a smirk as he said, "Really? Most of these people don't have that much." The country director countered, "Just because they don't have very much doesn't mean they don't struggle with materialism. They *long* to be rich."

---

[5] Ibid.

The Way Forward

Jesus declared, "Where your treasure is, there your heart will be also" (Matthew 6:21). Where you put your money indicates where you put your heart. Randy Alcorn updates Jesus' statement: "Show me your checkbook, your credit card statement...and I'll show you where your heart is."[6]

But where you put your money also determines where your heart will go. For example, you feel more invested in a project when you pour money, time and resources into it. In the same way, when you start investing your money into spiritual things, you begin to value spiritual things. That's why Paul instructs Timothy,

> Teach those who are rich in this world not to be proud and not to trust in their money, which is so unreliable. Their trust should be in God, who richly gives us all we need for our enjoyment. Tell them to use their money to do good. They should be rich in good works and generous to those in need, always being ready to share with others. By doing this they will be storing up their treasure as a good foundation for the future so that they may experience true life. (1 Timothy 6:17-19, NLT)

Simply forming a critique of materialism won't help you break free from its grip. You must replace it with something.

Materialism nearly wrecked my faith. For years, my spiritual mentor pleaded with me to renounce my drive to live for money and possessions. We studied passages, which warn about its dangers. We read Christian books about it. But all his efforts ricocheted off me.

On the one hand, I stubbornly insisted on living for money. On the other, I longed to live for God and serve him. I tried to convince myself I could do both. But Jesus' words kept ringing in my ears, "You can't serve both God and money. In time, you'll love one and hate the other." As a last ditch effort, my mentor suggested I give a small amount to God's work.

---

[6] Alcorn, *Money, Possessions, and Eternity*, 101.

At first I said, "I have all this credit card debt I need to pay. I'll start giving when I get rid of it." But he pointed out "If you use that line of reasoning, you'll never start giving. God tells us to put him first and trust him to take care of the rest." So I started giving a paltry amount. I spent more on fast food in a month than I gave. But something clicked when I started giving my money to God's work.

That small step of faith gradually changed my perspective. I no longer saw myself as an owner of my money and possessions, but as a steward of God's money and possessions. I stopped asking myself, "How much of my money do I want to give?" And I started asking myself, "How much of God's money do I plan to keep?"

This step of faith represented a landmark moment in my walk. I felt myself getting more excited about spiritual things as I invested my money in God's work. And over time, this excitement outstripped any thrill I got from a new purchase.

If you want to loosen materialism's hold on you, start by taking small steps toward generous giving. God doesn't care how much you give. He cares that you exercise faith.

For Further Discussion:

1. What are some signs that you're drawing a false sense of security from the money you've accumulated?
2. What are other practical steps we can take to loosen materialism's grip on us?

STEWARDING YOUR WEALTH

These days, you rarely hear people call someone a "steward." The Oxford English Dictionary defines a steward as, "a person employed to manage another's property, especially a large house or estate." The New Testament frequently uses this word to describe one aspect of our relationship to God. According to the Bible, God entrusted us with everything we have (1 Corinthians 4:7). And at the end of our lives, he will call us to account for what we did with it.

Often we resist seeing the world from this perspective. We tend to view our life like a library book; we act as if we own it even though it's on loan to us. Yet, when we take steps toward generous giving, God slowly transforms our outlook. We no longer see ourselves as the owner of our money and possessions. Instead, we view our money and possessions as a stewardship from God.

But for many of us, a new outlook won't fix our financial problems. Bad spending habits and poor financial decisions have thrown us into debt. We need practical advice for how to climb out of the financial hole we've dug for ourselves.

Luckily, Proverbs dispenses practical wisdom about debt, savings and lending. In this chapter, we'll narrow our focus to just debt and savings.[1]

Loans and Debt

Scripture warns us to steer clear of debt. For example, Proverbs pictures debt as an iron collar around the borrower's neck. "The rich rules over the poor, and the borrower *becomes* the lender's slave" (Proverbs 22:7, NASB). A few verses later, the wise man cautions us about defaulting on our debts. "If you lack the means to pay, your very bed will be snatched from under you" (Proverbs

---

[1] For an excellent discussion on lending and cosigning for loans, see Appendix C in Randy Alcorn's book *Money, Possessions, and Eternity*.

22:27). That's why the Apostle Paul insists, "Let no debt remain outstanding, except the continuing debt to love one another" (Romans 12:8). But putting ourselves in debt may create other problems.

Debt generates stress and anxiety. We sink deeper into our chair when we view our credit card statements. Waves of anxiety hit us when we get the mail and open one overdue notice after another. Fear grips us when creditors call to intimidate us.

Money problems may also put a strain on a marriage. It saps emotional energy from our relationships. Family counselors point to financial stress as a major source of conflict in marriages. It also plays a factor in many divorces.[2] How many Americans end up with everything they wanted, but wind up divorced and alienated from their children?

Like a stubborn clog, debt restricts our ability to give. It stands in the way of us giving when the Spirit prompts us. It ties up money we could invest in things containing eternal value. How much money could we release toward God's work if we managed to climb out of debt? Or to phrase it differently: How much could God do with the hundreds of dollars we throw at our debt each month?

Now when we talk about debt, it's important to distinguish between different kinds of debt. Certain types of debt can be more difficult to eliminate compared to others.

Credit Card Debt and Car Loans

Credit cards and car loans fall into the category of consumer debt. Consumer debt refers to debt you incur from purchasing goods you consume. Over time, these goods depreciate in value (e.g. clothes, electronics, shoes, etc.).

Credit cards often carry high interest rates compared to other types of debt. This makes them more difficult to pay off. On the

---

[2] D. G. Schramm (et. al). *Marriage in Utah: 2003 baseline statewide survey on marriage and divorce.* Salt Lake City: Utah Department of Workforce Services.

high end, credit card companies charge a 20% annual percentage rate. So if you racked up $3,000 in credit card debt you would pay $50 a month in interest alone. If you paid $100 a month, it would take you three-and-a-half years to pay off your credit card. But in the course of paying it off, it would cost you $1,193 in interest charges.

Car loans also land in the category of consumer debt, but they carry lower interest rates. Although most cars depreciate, purchasing a reliable car expands your employment opportunities. In some cases, you may even look to your car as a source of income (i.e. pizza delivery, taxi cab driver, etc.).

But let's face it. Most people don't purchase a car just to get from point A to point B. They buy a Mercedes because it's "engineered to move the human spirit." They sign the papers at the dealerships to get a BMW for the "sheer driving pleasure." Or people will finance a Volkswagen because it "relieves gas pain."

In our culture, a person's car contributes to their image. You hear people say, "I wouldn't be caught dead driving that thing." Or, "I'll never buy a minivan. It just doesn't scream punk rock." So they stretch their monthly budget to get a car that happens to match their personality.

If you put it all together, many Americans find themselves buried under a mountain of consumer debt. According to the Federal Reserve, the average household carries a $7,813 balance on their credit cards. However, that includes households with no debt. If you just count households with debt, the average rockets up to $16,140. In addition to this, Americans borrow an average of $28,381 to purchase a new car. And most Americans have at least two cars sitting in their garage. Therefore, if your family owns two brand new cars and carries the average credit card balance, you're sitting on $72,902 in consumer debt.

Student Loans

College costs continue to soar and they outpace inflation. For example, if you enrolled at Harvard, tuition and fees alone will cost you $45,278 a year.[3] That's 17 times more than the cost of tuition in 1971. If tuition rose at the same rate as inflation, Harvard's tuition would cost $15,189. Meanwhile, the cost for providing an education has remained stable.[4]

You might say, "Well, we're also talking about Harvard." Yet, tuition at public universities has also climbed at an alarming rate. From 2000-2013, the average tuition at a four-year public college rose by 87%. During that same period, the median income for middle class Americans grew by 24%.[5]

As a result, more and more students graduate chained to a large amount of debt. And over the last two decades, the average student loan debt has grown by a staggering amount. Mark Kantrowitz, an expert in student loans, points out,

> In 1993-94, about half of bachelor's degree recipients graduated with debt, averaging a little more than $10,000. This year, more than two-thirds of college graduates graduated with debt, and their average debt at graduation was about $35,000, tripling in two decades.[6]

And that's just the average. Those who graduated from a private college may owe twice as much.

After my wife finished her degree, she landed a job at a public library. She worked closely with a woman who recently completed

---

[3] This does not including room and board.

[4] "IPEDS Analytics: Delta Cost Project Database 1987-2012," The Delta Cost Project, Integrated Postsecondary Education Data System, https://nces.ed.gov/ipeds/deltacostproject/

[5] "Why does a college degree cost so much?" CNBC, last modified June 6, 2016, http://www.cnbc.com/2015/06/16/why-college-costs-are-so-high-and-rising.html

[6] "Why the Student Loan Crisis Is Even Worse Than People Think" Time Money, last modified January 11, 2016, http://time.com/money/4168510/why-student-loan-crisis-is-worse-than-people-think/

her graduate degree. As they were working one day, this woman shared that she was carrying an absurd amount of student loan debt. She quipped, "When I graduated with my master's degree, I bought a house. Now I have two mortgage payments." She earned her Master's of Library Science, but couldn't find a full-time job as a librarian. So she worked part-time while making an $1100/month student loan payment.

This new reality requires us to re-examine how we view a college education. We may need to weigh the income we could earn in a certain career field with the amount of student loan debt we will accrue. Maybe we should start at a community college and then transfer to a four-year college. Or maybe we should look at a public university instead of a private college to cut costs.

Some of us may need to ask ourselves if it's even worth going to college. Maybe it would make more sense to pursue a trade or a technical degree. I've encountered bright people who possessed the capacity to complete a four-year degree. But they didn't flourish in a classroom setting. I've also met some people who were earning more right out of high school than people who found jobs within their career field in college. It didn't make sense for them to go to college since their career contained a high earning potential.

Now I want to be crystal clear. I'm not suggesting people stop enrolling in college. I'm a college graduate. I earned a master's degree and my wife completed a bachelor's degree. But both of our parents paid for our tuition. Most people don't have that luxury. I'm simply suggesting an alternative to college.

Mortgages

There was a time when most financial experts would tell you that it's better to buy a home than to rent. You would hear people say, "When you rent, you're throwing your money away." Or, "You should buy a house. It's a good investment."

But everything changed when the housing market bubble burst in 2008, sending the US economy into the worst recession since the

Great Depression. Housing prices took a nosedive. According to economist Robert Shiller, it was the largest price drop in history.[7] People were underwater on their house, meaning their loan amount exceeded the value of their house.

This recession opened people's eyes to the benefits of renting. First, you aren't throwing your money away when you rent. You're paying for a place live. Second, home ownership requires you to pay for repairs and broken appliances. If you rent, you can call your landlord when a water pipe bursts in your apartment. As a homeowner, you call a local plumber and brace yourself for the worst. Third, it's usually cheaper to rent than to buy. In most major cities, your mortgage payment and property tax will exceed what you would pay in rent. Now I'm not against home ownership. I own a home. I'm simply challenging the notion that "it's always better to buy than to rent."

Some people suffer frequent financial headaches because their mortgage has put a stranglehold on their budget. They stretched their budget to get their "dream" home. It was right above their max budget, but they justified spending more by telling themselves, "We just had to have it."

In some cases, parents entice their children to buy too much house. They offer to help with a down payment or cosign for the loan. But an unplanned hospital visit or a loss of income threatens their ability to pay their bills.

Our decision to buy a home should include more than financial concerns. As followers of Christ, we seek to honor God in all we do. Purchasing a home represents a huge commitment that may impact your spiritual life. Here are few questions to turn over in your mind as you house hunt.

---

[7] Robert Schiller, "Home price drop is biggest ever," CNN Money, last modified January 29, 2008, http://money.cnn.com/2008/01/29/real_ estate/record_drop_home_prices/

1. Will the location of this house become a barrier to remaining highly involved in my spiritual community? Will it be too far away? Will the distance deter people from coming to see me?

2. Am I seeking to honor God with this purchase? You shouldn't buy a house just because you can afford it. Am I aiming to purchase a home that will meet my family's needs? Or am I trying to impress my friends and family? Will the layout allow me to host a small group?

3. Can I afford this house based on one income? Most young couples don't look far enough into the future when purchasing a home. Most people buy a home based on what they can afford with a dual income. Yet, everything changes when two or more kids appear in their lives. They soon discover that the cost of childcare devours most of their second income.[8]

Therefore, it may show some wisdom to buy a house based on one income. This will provide you flexibility for one parent to stay home with the kids. This will help you to avoid compromising what's best for your family.

Getting Out of Debt

Some of you feel overwhelmed by the amount of debt you're carrying. You feel helpless to climb out of the financial hole in which you've dug yourself. Let me offer four suggestions for clawing your way out of debt.

1. *Meet with a financial planner.* I don't claim to be a financial expert. And your financial situation may contain complicated issues. Thus, it may be wise to seek expert advice about your finances. Most churches offer personal finance workshops that will help you

---

[8] According to one Pew Research article, the average weekly child-care expenses –for families with working mothers– rose more than 70% from 1985 to 2011. Based on current figures, families paid an average of $12,000 a year for child-care. With two or more kids, most of a family's second income could go towards child-care. Drew Desilver, "Rising cost of child care may help explain recent increase in stay-at-home moms," Pew Research Center, last modified April 8, 2014, http://www.pewresearch.org/fact-tank/2014/04/08/rising-cost-of-child-care-may-help-explain-increase-in-stay-at-home-moms/

develop a budget and provide you with ways to dig yourself out of debt. Also, check to see if your church has set up a personal financial ministry. Our church calls our personal finance ministry GIFT, which stands for Generous Investments in Future Treasures. It helps people to gain control of their financial situation and maximizes their generosity.

2. *Differentiate your needs from your wants.* A couple of years ago, my four-year-old son Julius and I visited my friend. Julius played with my friend's kids while we stood around and talked. At one point, Julius walked up to my friend's daughter and strong-armed her for the toy she was holding. She walked up to us, with tears welling up in her eyes and her lower lip sticking out. I turned to Julius and said, "Give that toy back to her." Instantly, he started crying and throwing a fit. In a whiny voice he kept repeating, "I need this! I need this!" My friend's five-year-old son walked up and said, "Julius, you don't need that. You want it." I tried to hold back my laughter as my son slowly handed the toy back to her.

Some of us grew up without seeing the difference between our needs and wants. We watched our parents strain their budget because they "needed" a new sports car or "needed" a vacation house. Or maybe they spent their money wisely, but never helped us develop self-control in the area of spending.

As a result, we see an advertisement and tell ourselves, "I need a new pair of shoes." Or we walk past the electronics section of a store and it triggers the thought, "I need a new device." But what we meant to say was, "I *want* a new pair of shoes" or "I *want* this device." If you boil your basic needs down to a short list, it would consist of food, basic clothes and shelter. In some places, you might add reliable transportation.

So we can take our first step toward reducing debt by limiting our spending to things we need. We must train ourselves to exercise self-control and resist spending money on things we want. Or as my friend put it, "We need to start living at the *need* level, instead of at the *greed* level."

Some of us can see the difference between our needs and wants. But we find ways to justify our spending. Let me offer some common excuses we make to rationalize excessive spending.

"I'm getting a good deal"

Some people step into the trap of bargain shopping. They always manage to find a good deal, but they buy things they don't need. "Check it out," they say, "I got a good deal and saved a lot of money." But they bought something they didn't need. So they weren't actually saving money, they were spending money. The morning after Black Friday this year, one of my friends said, "I saved hundreds of dollars on Black Friday! I slept through it."

"I can afford it"

Just because we can afford something doesn't mean we should buy it. Again, we need to hit the pause button before making a purchase and ask ourselves, "Do I really need this?" Often, we're just upgrading something that already works.

Not to mention, we often don't budget for the extras we need for large purchases. For example, you go and purchase a High Definition TV. But then you get home and realize you need new cables and a different TV mount for it to work in your space. These add hundreds of dollars to your original purchase.

"I'm buying this because it's higher quality and will last longer"

I once overheard a girl say, "I'm going to buy these $300 hiking-boots. They're the same kind of boots people wear to climb Mount Everest." I had to hold myself back from turning to her and saying, "But you're going to use them to walk to class in three inches of snow."

Let's not fool ourselves. Most of the time, we don't buy things because they're higher quality. We buy them for the name brand and the status they bring.

"I'll save money in the long run"

Often, we're not looking to save money; we just want to buy something new. Take for instance, buying a new car for its improved gas mileage. We convince ourselves that we'll save money without doing the math. Randy Alcorn dismantles the faulty reasoning behind this view.

> Studies in The Wall Street Journal prove that it's far less expensive to maintain a used car than buy a new one. "The cheapest car anyone can ever own is always the car they presently own," and "The longer a car is driven, the cheaper it becomes to operate." Yet, when we get the "car bug," we make irrational decisions. A man "on a tight budget" tried to explain how he'd made a wise decision buying a brand-new car that got forty miles per gallon to replace his old paid-for car (still running fine) that got only twenty-five miles per gallon. This man had committed himself to paying $270 per month in order to "save" $30 per month. He was coming out $240 per month behind. Given the high depreciation on his new car, by the time he was finished with his payments it would be worth little more than his old, fully depreciated car. Yet, his desire for the new car was so strong it overrode all reason, convincing him he'd made a wise "investment."[9]

3. *Cultivate contentment.* We live in a culture that breeds discontent. Advertisements flood our screens, arousing and nurturing these feelings. Companies brand their products, selling us a lifestyle and promise of happiness.

Our culture stamps out consumers who believe only more will make them happy. Advertising firms seek to capture, own and brand us from a very young age. According to the authors of *Affluenza,*

> "Corporations are recognizing that the consumer lifestyle starts younger and younger," explains Joan Chiaramonte, who does market research for the Roper Starch polling firm. "If you wait to reach children with your product until they're eighteen years

---

[9] Alcorn, *Money, Possessions, and Eternity,* 317.

of age, you probably won't capture them." From 1980 to 2004 the amount spent on children's advertising in America rose from $100 million to $15 billion a year, a staggering 15,000 percent! In her book, *Born to Buy*, Juliet Schor points out that children are now also used effectively by marketers to influence their parents' purchases of big-ticket items, from luxury automobiles to resort vacations and even homes.[10]

For many of us, discontentment has brought a steady stream of debt into our lives. According to Scripture, only contentment can plug this hole. The book of Hebrews tells us, "Keep your lives free from the love of money and be content with what you have" (13:5). Some might say, "Well, I'll be content once I get that new bike." Or "I'll be happy when we finally remodel our outdated kitchen." But contentment appears to have no connection with how much you have.

The author of Hebrews supplies us with the basis for contentment, "*because* God has said, 'Never will I leave you; never will I forsake you'" (Hebrews 13:5b-6). Contentment comes from seeing your security in Christ. When we adopt an attitude of contentment, we're suggesting God has provided us with all we need.

So how do you develop contentment? I've found that forming a habit of thanking God helps me feel content. When I list all the things God has given me, it suppresses my desire for more. Also, it helps to take a break from spending. I find that spending money feeds my desire for more.

4. *Adopt a lifestyle of simple living.* "Simple living" describes a lifestyle aimed at scaling back spending. People who embrace this way of life seek to live at the level of their needs, rather than their wants. To some, it may include reducing their possessions –getting

---

[10] John de Graaf, David Wann, and Thomas H. Naylor, *Affluenza: How Overconsumption Is Killing Us – and How to Fight Back* (Oakland, CA: Berrett-Koehler Publishers, 2014), 45-46.

rid of all the stuff they don't need. Some even choose to downsize their home, which helps limit the stuff they can warehouse.

Adopting a lifestyle of simple living enables you to pay down your debt quicker. Over time, you'll grow to enjoy finding new and creative ways to save money.

I recall the first time I met my spiritual mentor. My eyes widened as I watched him rattle up the driveway in his 15-year-old Honda Civic to teach a Bible study.

One time, I asked him if I could catch a ride with him to the convenience store. I jumped into his car and started sneering about how his car was falling apart. He looked at me and said, "Dude, what's wrong with my car? It has a CD player. It has air conditioning. It eventually gets up to 75 miles per hour. And I get 35 miles to the gallon. This car is awesome!"

He drove that car five more years until it started to leak gasoline. But he drove it for another year because he said it "got such good gas mileage." He calculated that even with a gas leak, he still got 30 miles to the gallon. He didn't seem to care that his car was a rolling Molotov cocktail.

As a young believer, I remember telling myself, "I'd never be caught dead driving that car." Each time I made fun of him for his crappy car, he would eagerly defend it. He would recite the list all of its amazing features, "It's got a CD player, air conditioning..." I would just laugh. It was almost like a game for him, to see how long he could keep his car alive. He never worried about getting dents in his car or someone opening their car door into his. It was one less thing to worry about. In fact, he might've describe those dings and dents as "patina," adding charm to his car.

My mentor never portrayed simple living as a painful sacrifice. He always made it seem like you could find a cheaper off-brand version of the same quality. Whenever we'd watch a game on TV, he'd howl in laugher at commercials, "So a Subaru brought that dad and his daughter closer together? So if I wear that deodorant, girls will think I'm hot?" He made simple living seem fun and countercultural.

Up to that point, I had never met anyone who lived simply. I met people who didn't have much and were ashamed of it. But the believers I encountered made simple living seem cool. And they seemed happier than people who possessed far more.

Saving and Hoarding

Proverbs commends those who save, "In the house of the wise are stores of choice food and oil, but a foolish man devours all he has" (Proverbs 21:20). The wise plan with the future in mind. According to Randy Alcorn, saving avoids "presuming upon others to assume responsibility for our future needs."[11]

Proverbs directs us to learn financial principles from nature. "Go to the ant, you sluggard; consider its ways and be wise! It has no commander, no overseer or ruler, yet it stores its provisions in summer and gathers its food at harvest" (Proverbs 6:6-8). I used to keep bees as a hobby. Spring and early summer brought the heaviest nectar flow. Some afternoons, I would sit and watch thousands of bees fly in and out of my hives. The workers were collecting nectar from flowers and storing honey. During a good year, a colony of bees could build a store of 80-100 pounds of honey in just two months. That much honey can sustain a large hive through the harshest Ohio winter. It amazed me that they were preparing for something eight months away.

In our culture, very few people save. According to one study, a third of Americans haven't saved any money for emergencies.[12] Another study discovered that 62% of Americans have less than $1,000 in their saving account and 20% didn't even have a savings account.[13] Although this study doesn't account for retirement or investments, it provides a window into people's saving habits.

---

[11] Alcorn, *Money, Possessions, and Eternity*, 333.

[12] "Millions of Americans have little to no money saved," USA Today, last modified March 31, 2015, http://www.usatoday.com/story/money/personal finance/2015/03/31/millions-of-americans-have-no-money-saved/70680904/

[13] "62% of Americans Have Under $1,000 in Savings, Survey Finds," Go Banking Rates, last modified October 5, 2015, http://www.gobankingrates.com

Most financial experts suggest saving three months' worth of living expenses. This will provide you a buffer if your employer lays you off. You should set aside money for ongoing maintenance (i.e. car repair) and upcoming expenses (i.e. your child's college education, family vacations, home repairs, etc.). And we should put money away for retirement if we're working within our career field.[14]

Even though it's wise to save, it poses a danger to those who gravitate toward hoarding. The wise view savings as a life raft, keeping them afloat during a financial storm. Fools hoard their money to gain a feeling of security only for death to snatch it away (Luke 12:18-21). Worry and anxiety drive their compulsion to hoard money. They aren't saving for a rainy day. They're saving for a rainy decade. Instead of entrusting themselves to God, they look to money as their rescuer.

Putting it altogether

The great English preacher and founder of the Methodist movement, John Wesley, famously said, "Make as much as you can, save as much as you can, and give as much as you can."[15] Once you get a leash on your out-of-control spending, you'll start finding extra money popping up in your checking account each month. That's what happened to me. Once this happens, it will open up new possibilities.

But before you develop a savings plan or start looking for investment options, put first things first. Don't determine what you're going to save and then give God what's left. Jesus taught, "Seek first His kingdom and His righteousness, and all these things will be added to you" (Matthew 6:33). Plan what you will give first

---

/savings-account/62-percent-americans-under-1000-savings-survey-finds/

[14] For an excellent and challenging view of retirement, see Randy Alcorn's chapter on Saving, Retiring, and Insuring, in his book *Money, Possessions, and Eternity.*

[15] John Wesley, *The Works of the Reverend John Wesley, A.M. Volume I* (New York: T. Mason and G. Lane, 1840), 446.

and *then* save the rest. When you set aside your giving first, you're taking steps toward prioritizing God and his purposes.

Questions to ask yourself when making a purchase

I want to leave you with some questions my friends and I generated, which you can ask yourself while making a purchase.[16]

- How often will I use this item? (e.g. specialized tools, backpacking equipment, etc.)
- Can I borrow this item from someone?
- How did I get by without this item?
- How did people in the past get by without this item (i.e. A new cooler just hit the market, which can keep food cold for seven days. How in the world did people take fishing/hunting trips before this cooler existed?)?
- Can I buy this item used?
- If I'm upgrading, is it necessary? Or does the existing system function well?
- Can I save up for this item? If I want it that bad, am I willing to wait while I save?
- Will this item be an asset or liability to my spiritual life? Will it help me serve God better or distract me from serving God?
- Are there ongoing costs associated with this item (i.e. refills, licenses, subscriptions, maintenance)? Factor this in the overall cost.
- Subscriptions and Memberships – How often would I need to use this service, to make it worth it? Do I use it that often (i.e. Amazon Prime, Netflix, Spotify, gym membership)?
- If I'm replacing something that's broken, how much would it cost to repair it?
- What was the thing I wanted so badly six months ago that I rarely use?
- Would I be embarrassed if someone who wasn't familiar with this sport or hobby discovered how much I paid for it?

---

[16] Thanks to my good friends Scott Arter and Scott Risley.

- Will this make me stand out even among worldly peers? Will worldly people envy this purchase?

- How could I impact God's kingdom with this money?

- Should I buy an expensive, high quality item or a cheaper version?

- Is this an item I will use regularly or occasionally (i.e. mattress, shoes vs. fishing pole, items for travel)?

- If I'm getting interested in a new hobby or sport, do I need to buy the most expensive equipment? How many items sit in my closet because of hobbies I quit? Can I borrow equipment from a friend until I'm confident it's something I want to pursue?

- Can I buy this item at a thrift store instead of buying it new (i.e. 99¢ tie that I can throw away if I dunk it into a bowl of soup)?

- Can I purchase it used? If it truly "lasts a lifetime," I should be able to buy a quality used one.

- Am I likely to lose this item (i.e. a travel mug, winter gloves, expensive fountain pen)?

FIGHTING FOR FRIENDSHIP

Our circle of friends keeps shrinking. According to sociologist Lynn Smith-Lovin, nearly 50% of Americans report they discuss important matters with either one person or no one at all. And this includes family members!

In recent decades, the number of people who say they can turn to at least one non-family member dropped from 80% to 57%. Even more concerning, those who reported they had *no one* to talk to about important matters nearly tripled.[1]

The Importance of Friendship

To most, the need for friendship appears self-evident. Yet, some of us have lived in isolation for so long that it's hard to see the urgency in building them. Let me provide three reasons why we need friendship.

First, God designed the need for friendship into our human architecture. According to the Bible, the first man enjoyed perfect fellowship with God. And yet, God saw man's longing for human connection. In Genesis 2:18, God declared, "It's not good for man to be alone." In fact, new research links loneliness with a higher risk of death.[2] Brigham Young University released a study showing that feelings of isolation increased the risk of death by 26%. Even worse, living alone increased a person's risk by 32%.

Second, following Christ requires us to love people and build close friendships. Sometimes you'll hear people say, "I'm good with God, but I really don't like people." That's impossible. According to

---

[1] Lynn Smith-Lovin, "Social Isolation in America: Changes in Core Discussion Networks over Two Decades," *American Sociological Review*, vol. 71 (June: 2006), 353–375.

[2] Julianne Holt-Lunstad, "Loneliness and Social Isolation as Risk Factors for Mortality: A Meta-Analytic Review" in *Perspectives of Psychological Science 2015*, Vol. 10 (2) 227-237.

the Bible, you can't claim to love God and fail to love people (1 John 4:7, 8). If you love God, then you will adopt his love for people.

Third, it's impossible to fulfill the "one another" passages without close friendships. The "one another" passages refer to biblical instructions such as "encourage one another," "confess to one another" and "bear one another's burdens." The Bible contains as many as 60 one another passages. They depict a vibrant spiritual community, which remains out of reach for those who won't commit to deepening their friendships. After all, how can we bear others' burdens if we barely know them? Would we confess our sins to someone we don't trust? This kind of depth will require more than two hours a week on Sunday morning. It will call for us to carve out significant time from our schedule.

Modern Challenges to Friendship

Sacrifice and effort alone won't guarantee good friendships. As modern Americans, we face several hurdles to building deep friendships.

Individualism

American individualism stands in the way of us enjoying deep friendships. It tells us to rely on ourselves and to refuse help. It pushes us to pursue success and self-expansion at all costs. It says that people don't have the right to dive into our personal matters, insisting that they should mind their own business. As a result, most Americans feel a gnawing sense of loneliness.

And yet, we yearn for the very things we resist. We long to open up with the people we push away. We look longingly upon friendships we left behind in order to pursue money or a career. And we suffer in silence because our pride blocks us from asking for help.

If we seek to build good friendships, we must reject our world's values and embrace God's values. We must spurn individualism and accept God's design for us.

Life Transitions

Life transitions act as a furnace, either refining or consuming our friendships. Recent studies show that college-aged people spend the most time with friends, logging 10-25 hours a week with them.[3] A college schedule gives you the flexibility to hang out with friends, from all-nighters at the library to crashing house parties on campus.

But when career demands, marriage and small children enter your life, it's no longer possible to "find time" for your friends. With a thousand things clamoring for your attention, you "make time" for what's important.

Life transitions also test how much we value friendship. For example, young adults enjoy denser friendship networks. When you're young, most of your friends live in town or go to your school. But as people move away for college or work, their network fans out. In a recent study, Andrew Ledbetter, a professor of communications at TCU conducted a study following pairs of best friends for 19 years. His research found that participants moved an average of 5.8 times after college. By year 19, very few pairs lived within 50 miles of each other with an average distance of 895 miles between friends.[4]

Our friendship will undergo testing at certain stages of life. And if we don't recommit ourselves to our friends, we'll end up drifting from them.

Information Technology

In the last two decades, information technology has changed the way we interact with our friends. Internet access allows us to stay

---

[3] The 2014 American Time Use Study found that people between 20-24 years old spent the most time socializing each day. Bureau of Labor Statistics, U.S. Department of Labor, *The Economics Daily*, "Time spent in leisure activities in 2014, by gender, age, and educational attainment," last modified June 29, 2015, http://www.bls.gov/opub/ted/2015/time-spent-in-leisure-activities-in-2014-by-gender-age-and-educational-attainment.htm

[4] Andrew Ledbetter, 'Forecasting "friends forever": A longitudinal investigation of sustained closeness between best friends,' *Personal Relationships*, 14 (2007), 343–350.

connected with friends living thousands of miles away. Instead of writing a letter to our friend Elaina –who lives in Paraguay– we can video chat her. Hand written letters provide a fraction of the interaction you can obtain from video chat. It may take two weeks to see how Elaina responds to our letter, whereas video chat enables us to see her facial expressions and hear her laugh in real time.

Fresh studies suggest mobile phones, social media and networked video games play a vital role in how teens interact. According to Pew Research, the majority of teens text message their friends every day.[5] When teens say, "I talked to so-and-so the other day," there's no way to tell if they're describing a text conversation or if they saw that person at school. For boys, video games play a crucial role in maintaining friendships. The majority (78%) felt like online gaming strengthened existing relationships.

But does increased interaction lead to authentic relating? Most teens claim they felt more "connected" through social media (83%). Yet, the majority (76%) said that people seem "less real" on social media and 40% of teens report feeling pressure to curate flattering or popular content.[6]

Sherry Turkle, professor of Social Studies of Science and Technology at MIT, uncovers the appeal of social media and text:

When I ask people "What's wrong with having a conversation?" People say, "It takes place in real time and you can't control what you're going to say." So that's the bottom line. Texting, email, posting, all of these things let us present the self we want to be. We get to edit, and that means we get to delete, and that

---

[5] 55% spend time every day text messaging friends. Amanda Lenhart (et. al), "Teens, Technology and Friendships." Pew Research, August 6, 2015, http://www.pewinternet.org/2015/08/06/teens-technology-and-friendships/

[6] Ibid. Notice, I didn't say in person. Teenagers view interacting through networked video games and texting as their primary way of relating to their friends. 59% of teens who play online with other use voice connection when they play.

means we get to retouch, the face, the voice, the flesh, the body –not too little, not too much, just right.[7]

You might be saying to yourself, "Isn't that a bit negative?" Or to quote comedian Stephen Colbert, "Don't all those little tweets, don't all those little sips of online communication, add up to one big gulp of real conversation?" I'd say social media, texting and email serve as useful tools to connect with friends. But they can never serve as a substitute for face-to-face relating. Turkle concludes:

> Human relationships are rich and they're messy and they're demanding. And we clean them up with technology. And when we do, one of the things that can happen is that we sacrifice conversation for mere connection.[8]

Some research even suggests our devices impair our ability to relate. In 2014, psychologist Yalda Uhls ran a field experiment to see if face-to-face relating improved people's ability to identify emotions. She selected 50 children to spend a few days at an outdoor camp. The catch: they had to leave their phones and tablets at home. After five days, Uhls asked campers to identify an emotional state from photographs and videos. She conducted the same experiment on a control group. The results: campers identified emotions *significantly* better than the control group.[9] What happened? These students spent time relating to one another without the distraction of a device. Deep relating requires us to pay close attention and to put ourselves in someone else's place. Turns out, it's easier to do that without a device in your hand.

In another study, most adults (82%) felt that people who used their cellphone in a social setting hurt conversation. Yet, nearly all

---

[7] Sherry Turkle, "Connected, but alone?" TED talk, February 2012.

[8] Ibid.

[9] Yalda Uhls, "Five days at outdoor education camp without screens improves preteen skills with nonverbal emotion cues" *Computers in Human Behavior* Volume 39 (October 2014): 387–392.

of them (89%) admitted to pulling out their phone at a recent gathering![10] Turkle offers a diagnosis:

> We're getting used to a new way of being alone together. People want to be with each other, but also elsewhere –connected to all the different places they want to be. People want to customize their lives. They want to go in and out of all the places they are because the thing that matters most to them is control over where they put their attention.[11]

Mobile devices place control firmly in our hands. If we grow bored with a conversation, we can opt out and talk to someone else. Turkle argues that we feel drawn to our devices because they satisfy three gratifying desires. "One, that we can put our attention wherever we want it to be; two, that we will always be heard; and three, that we will never have to be alone."[12]

But our ability to be alone –without notifications and alerts– aids reflection. Reflection furnishes us with insight, which provides substance to our conversations. We can't build satisfying friendships simply by exchanging soundbites and facts.

As mentioned earlier, digital communication works better for maintaining certain types of relationships. It helps us stay connected with loved ones living in different cities or countries. It keeps us updated about old friends with whom we've lost contact.

But digital communication can only supply a certain amount of closeness. To attain further depth, you need more than an online presence. Close friendships require face-to-face interactions. Information technology strengthens existing close friendships, but it can never serve as a substitute for "real" relating.

---

[10] "Americans' Views on Mobile Etiquette," Pew Research Center, last modified August 8, 2015, http://www.pewinternet.org/2015/08/26/americans-views-on-mobile-etiquette/

[11] Sherry Turkle, "Connected, but alone?" TED talk, February 2012.

[12] Ibid.

Qualities of a Good Friend

Nearly two dozen proverbs describe how we should interact with our "neighbor." Like any word, *neighbor* contains a wide range of meaning. In Hebrew, it can refer to either a person who lives nearby or a close friend. In most cases, Proverbs uses it to describe the way friends should relate to one another.

The book of Proverbs lists qualities found in a good friend. It both urges us to search for these qualities *in* a friend and to acquire these qualities *as* a friend. Let's take a moment to look through this list.

Show Consistency

Proverbs tells us that the world contains many fair-weather friends. They hobnob with the rich, hoping it will open up new opportunities. But when their friend's wealth dries up, they vanish like dew on a summer morning (19:4, 6, 7). Yet, some friends "stick closer" than a brother or sister (18:24). They remain loyal during life's highs and lows (17:17).

Before I met Christ, my friendships never lasted. They always followed the same pattern. I would befriend someone, we would hang out every day and then something would happen. One of us would get a girlfriend and disappear or we'd get into an argument that would fracture our friendship. Or we would simply drift apart. It was as if someone slapped a one-year expiration date on all of my friendships.

However, everything changed when I received Christ. It transformed both my life and my relationships. Unlike past friendships, I was able to overcome conflict with my Christian friends. Christ gave me both the basis for forgiveness and the motivation to reconcile (Colossians 3:13; Matthew 5:23-24).

Christ also laid a new foundation for my friendships. They no longer stand on common interests or experiences. God has fastened my friendships to something secure. Scripture teaches that the moment we receive Christ, God unites us with him. By extension,

God unites us with other believers (Ephesians 4:3). Thus, our unity rests on something stable, unmovable.

Speak Truth

Faithful friends speak truth to one another even when it hurts. The wise man tells us, "Faithful are the wounds of a friend, but deceitful are the kisses of an enemy" (Proverbs 27:6, NASB).

People in our culture hesitate to speak honestly with their friends. The widespread moral relativism in our culture has left people without a voice to declare something "wrong." You'll overhear people say, "If they think they're right, who am I to say it is wrong?"

As followers of Christ, we don't look inward to determine right from wrong. We turn to an external source for guidance, God's written word. Scripture reveals God's moral will to us. It bends and shapes our values to resemble God's values. Thus, Scripture gives us the basis to speak truth in love to our friends (Ephesians 4:15).

But there's more to speaking truth than pointing out problems. Speaking honestly includes encouraging our friends. At times, a friend will sink into despair because God uncovered a sin problem in their lives. Or they feel grief-stricken because they're facing suffering. In each case, God calls on us to urge our friends forward, clinging to the truth.

Give Wise Counsel

Friends should lean on each other for good advice. Proverbs 27:9 says, "The heartfelt counsel of a friend is as sweet as perfume" (NLT). We stumble across many confusing situations as we try to walk with God. He promises to give us wisdom if we ask him for it. And he will likely answer us by sending a trusted friend to give us advice. I can't count the number of times I've been confused and decided to pursue a direction, only to have God redirect me through a friend's wise counsel.

In other cases, God uses a healthy clash of personalities to hone our perspective. "As iron sharpens iron, so a friend sharpens a friend" (Proverbs 27:17, NLT). At times, I find myself in sharp disagreement with a close friend over a confusing ministry issue. But after hammering it out with him, I often emerge with a better grasp of the issue or a refined plan.

Show Relational Awareness

A lack of relational awareness can ruin a friendship. For example, some people impose their presence upon their friends. If their number appears on Caller ID, their friends will roll their eyes while hitting the ignore button. Proverbs 25:17 advises, "Seldom set foot in your neighbor's house –too much of you, and he will hate you."

Others have developed anti-social habits, which irritate their friends. "A loud and cheerful greeting early in the morning will be taken as a curse!" (27:14, NLT). During college, I lived with some unusual people. For instance, one of my roommates would grocery shop and stock up on two months' worth of frozen pizzas. He would come home and stuff both of our freezers full. When you would peek into the freezer, a flood of pizzas would spill out of it. We would have to wait for him to eat some of his pizzas before we could put anything into the freezer.

Another roommate in college would take forever to use the bathroom. We would hear water running as we pounded on the door to get him to hurry. We pestered him for months to tell us what he was doing in there. Finally, he broke down. He couldn't use the bathroom unless he took off every article of clothing and turned on the shower!

Although some habits contain a certain amount of charm, others drive people away. For instance, one of my friends would correct your grammar and pronunciation while you were speaking. Yet, he seemed unaware of how he was offending people. In these cases, we may need to reflect our friend's behavior back to him or her. "I know you're joking when you make sarcastic comments, but people take them as cynical jabs. I'm not sure that's what you want to communicate."

Still others display a lack of awareness that seems downright cruel. "Singing cheerful songs to a person with a heavy heart is like taking someone's coat in cold weather or pouring vinegar in a wound" (Proverbs 25:20, NLT). By comparison, thoughtful friends can read a situation and provide a fitting response.

Few and Close

According to Proverbs 18:24, "A man of many companions may come to ruin, but there is a friend who sticks closer than a brother." It's possible to surround yourself with people and still feel alone. Just as a thriving plant requires deep roots, so spiritual friendships require depth.

A few years ago, I visited my hometown of Chicago. While in town, I caught up with an old friend from high school named Vic. Vic and I hung out almost every day during high school. We would skip class and roam around our neighborhood, getting into trouble.

When I first met Vic, he was going through some hard times. His mom lost her battle with cancer. Yet, he never mentioned to me that his mom passed. I heard about it from our other friends. For some reason we never talked about it.

As the night went on and the conversation started to wind down, I felt the Spirit nudging me to say something about it. So I said, "You know when we first met, I knew your mom passed away. I regret never asking you about it. I'm sorry I wasn't there for you."

Thankfully, God has taught me how to cultivate deep friendships. Like a father prodding a fearful son, God spurs me to loosen my tongue and open up with my friends. He showed me that faithful friends don't just spend time with each other; they talk to each other.

Don't Influence You to Sin

Proverbs 12:26 warns, "The righteous choose their friends carefully, but the way of the wicked leads them astray" (NET). The fact that God changes us from the inside-out doesn't excuse us from taking external precautions. We're more prone to people's influence than we like to admit.

Sometimes even good intentions lead us into temptation. For example, we may try to reach out to one of our non-Christian friends. But instead of exerting influence on him/her for God, they influence us to compromise our faith. We should heed Paul's warning in 1 Corinthians 15:33: "Bad company corrupts good character."

According to Proverbs, we may even co-opt new patterns of sin from our friends. "Do not make friends with a hot-tempered man, do not associate with one easily angered, or you may learn his ways and get yourself ensnared" (Proverbs 22:24-25).

This also works in the opposite direction. Spending time with spiritual people stokes our fire for God. Proverbs 13:20 makes this connection: "Walk with the wise and become wise; associate with fools and get in trouble" (NLT).

A Blueprint for Success

First Samuel gives us one of the best examples of friendship in the Bible, the friendship between David and Jonathan. Their relationship rested upon a solid spiritual foundation. Both David and Jonathan committed their lives to following God. They found each other in this context.

By comparison, most American Christians would say you have your "church" friends and then you have your "real" friends. But the Bible doesn't draw this distinction. David and Jonathan forged their friendship through their relationship with God.

Thus, their friendship serves as a blueprint for spiritual friendships. David and Jonathan's relationship provides us with four essential elements of lasting friendships. Let's examine each.

Gave of Themselves Sacrificially

David and Jonathan rooted their friendship in sacrificial love. David met Jonathan in Saul's court while clutching Goliath's severed head. Right away, God knit Jonathan's soul to David's soul. Or to use a more modern term, they "hit it off."

But their friendship didn't last because they "clicked" with each other. Sacrificial love served as an epoxy, which held David and Jonathan's friendship together. Samuel tells us that Jonathan loved David as he loved himself (1 Samuel 18:1).

Centuries later, Jesus would exalt this kind of love, "Greater love has no one than this, that he lay down his life for his friends" (John 15:13). Jesus not only taught this kind of love; he displayed it on the cross.

Often we look for a friend to love us and to meet our needs. But the Bible tells us we're approaching friendship from the wrong starting point. We should look to meet others' needs, as we trust God to meet our needs.

Remained Committed to Their Friendship

David and Jonathan entered their friendship with a solemn pact and they remained committed to each other (1 Samuel 18:3-4). On two separate occasions, they reaffirmed their commitment (1 Samuel 20:23). This resulted in a life-long friendship.

In the same way, we must fight to maintain our friendships. As we get older, our lives grow more complicated. Marriage, children and career consume more of our time and attention. And our friendships undergo entropy as we drift toward comfort. Like David and Jonathan, we must reaffirm our commitment to our friendships. Otherwise, we'll slowly sail toward isolation.

Made Sacrifices in Every Area for Their Friendship

For instance, Jonathan was willing to part with his possessions to serve David. Samuel tells us that when David and Jonathan made their solemn pact, "Jonathan sealed the pact by taking off his robe and giving it to David, together with his tunic, sword, bow, and belt" (1 Samuel 18:4, NLT). Jonathan's gifts prepared David for both court and battle.[13]

---

[13] Chafin and Ogilvie, *Preacher's Commentary*, 140.

They also shared their emotions with each other. In 1 Samuel 20, Jonathan arranged a secret meeting with David to warn him about Saul's murderous plot. As they parted ways, "Both of them were in tears as they embraced each other and said good-bye, especially David" (1 Samuel 20:41, NLT).

David and Jonathan didn't show love in selective ways. They didn't say, "I don't need to tell people how much I care about them. They should just know that I care." David and Jonathan extended themselves in every area for the other's well-being.

Did What Was Best for Each Other

At times, they offered each other needed encouragement. For example, Jonathan assured David that his father wouldn't lay a hand on him. He reminded David that God anointed him the next king of Israel (1 Samuel 23:16-17).

At other times, David and Jonathan helped each other see the truth. When Saul's jealousy turned murderous, David challenged Jonathan to see it for himself (1 Samuel 20). It was painful for Jonathan, but it strengthened their bond.

David and Jonathan's friendship captures the type of love you should see in your spiritual friendships. And it fits with a definition of love I heard as a young Christian. Biblical love describes "a commitment to give of yourself in every area, for the good of another."[14] David and Jonathan's friendship embodied all of these elements of love.

Lasting Friendships

Sadly, death caused a temporary disruption to David and Jonathan's friendship. Jonathan lost his life in battle alongside his father. When David heard about Jonathan's death, he composed a funeral song to pay tribute to his friend:

Oh, how the mighty heroes have fallen in battle! Jonathan lies dead on the hills. How I weep for you, my brother Jonathan!

---

[14] I drew this from Dr. Ralph Ankeman's lecture entitled *Love Therapy*.

Oh, how much I loved you! And your love for me was deep, deeper than the love of women! (2 Samuel 1:25-26, NLT)

God will provide us with lasting spiritual friendships as he did David. And the hope of our salvation guarantees we will enjoy them for the rest of eternity.

For more than 15 years, my close friends and I drove to North Carolina to spend a week at the beach. Over the years, I've built incredible memories there. But by far, my first trip stands out as the most memorable.

One evening, my friends and I were on the deck overlooking the ocean with cold beverages. We were laughing and telling stories as the sun set. As we were talking, something unusual happened. I felt surrounded by God's love as I sat there with my close friends. In that moment, I felt real joy and contentment. It was as if God was giving me a glimpse of eternity.

For all those years, I assumed the scenery made our vacation special. Each year was the same. We would arrive at the beach after driving through the night. The front door would swing open. We would drop our bags, rush to the back deck and look at the spectacular view of the ocean.

This year, we did something different. We vacationed at a lake house in Tennessee. To my surprise, God gave me another one of these rare experiences.

This experience helped crystallize for me what will bring us the most joy in heaven. I feel certain God will create stunning landscapes and scenery for us on the new earth. And I'm excited to see what they will look like. But now, I'm most excited about *who* will occupy heaven, not *what* it will contain.

For Further Discussion:

1. What are other ways information technology deters our ability to relate or build deep friendships?
2. What are some ways we can develop more relational awareness and sophistication?

3. What are some symptoms that indicate we have shallow friendships?

GODLY DISCIPLINE

Our culture has blurred the line between discipline and abuse. In fact, people will sometimes use the words *discipline* and *abuse* interchangeably.

Experts warn of the harmful effects of discipline. As a result, the practice of discipline has fallen out of favor in our current culture. Yet, Scripture takes a counter-cultural stance on this topic. According to the Bible, love often requires us to discipline.

The Need for Discipline

Sin clouds our minds. We talk ourselves into believing we know what's best. We resist God's attempts to give us input, insisting we do things our way. However, this often leaves us feeling unhappy and unfulfilled. In some cases, it plunges us into a destructive way of life.

That's why God steps in and provides loving correction. He loves us and refuses to watch us ruin our lives. He gently prunes away our sin and character flaws so we can bear more fruit (John 15:2; Galatians 5:22-23). His discipline aims to produce a harvest of righteousness in us (Hebrews 12:11). It also brings peace. When discipline succeeds, rebellion ceases. It removes the blockage that restricts the flow of intimacy between God and us.

Now we should be careful not to mistake discipline for punishment. Punishment doesn't attempt to correct. It looks to exact justice. If someone commits a crime, he or she must pay for it. On the other hand, discipline doesn't seek to punish. It aims to transform. As followers of Christ, we shouldn't tremble at the thought of God's judgment. God poured his wrath out onto his son Jesus. That means discipline contains a redemptive purpose. God disciplines us for our good, as a loving father disciplines his child. That's why Solomon urges us, "Do not reject the discipline of the LORD or loathe His reproof, for whom the LORD loves He reproves, even as a father *corrects* the son in whom he delights" (Proverbs 3:11-12, NASB).

God's discipline also proves our adoption as his son or daughter. Right after I got married, my wife and I traveled to Machu Picchu (the ancient Incan citadel). On our way home, bad weather delayed our flight. Tired and frustrated, we sat at the gate and tried to get some sleep. But a woman unleashed her out-of-control son on people at the gate. For hours, he ran in circles around the gate screaming and opening people's luggage. Meanwhile, his mother seemed oblivious to her son terrorizing other travelers; at times, she even dozed off. People kept shooting glances at her, as if to say, "Get your kid under control."

Now that I have two boys under the age of five, I don't even flinch when I see another person's kid throwing a fit. At this point, it just sounds like white noise to me. But at the time, I wanted to pull that kid aside and say, "Hey! You need to calm down. Why don't you sit down and relax" (as I often say to my 2-year-old). But I couldn't. Why? Because he wasn't my son. In the same way, the presence of God's discipline certifies our adoption.

God's discipline comes to us in a variety of ways. At times, he takes a direct approach by confronting us through his written word. At other times, he allows suffering to enter our lives (Hebrews 12). But most of the time, he offers loving correction through Christian friends and family.

For the rest of this chapter, we'll direct our attention to the latter since the book of Proverbs talks most about this form discipline. But before we go any further, let's address a question some people may be kicking around in their head: "How can we presume to tell people what they should and shouldn't do?"

Basis for Correction

People in our culture take a dim view of discipline. People roll their eyes when they overhear somebody suggesting they "know" what's best in the area of sexuality or morality. After all, no one holds a monopoly on truth. So when you tell someone what he or she ought to do, you put your arrogance on display.

But as followers of Christ, we aren't puffing out our chests and telling people we know better. We're not suggesting, we've figured things out. God lays out his design for us through his written word, the Bible. Proverbs 6:23 plainly states, "For these commands are a lamp, this teaching is a light, and the corrections of discipline are the way to life." Thus, God's instruction serves as a basis for our correction.

Scripture gives us our moral bearing. It orients us to what's right and wrong. For example, Paul says, 'I would not have come to know sin except through the Law; for I would not have known about coveting if the Law had not said, "Do not covet"' (Romans 7:7). If God didn't reveal his moral will, we would stagger from sea to sea searching for it. Yet, we would never find it.

Sin has damaged our moral compass. We need an external objective reference point whereby we can judge our thoughts, attitudes and actions. When pilots fly in poor weather conditions, they're prone to what flight experts call "spatial disorientation." Spatial disorientation occurs when a pilot can't see a visible horizon and tries to navigate by his senses. Without an objective point of reference, the pilot literally can't tell "which way is up." His perception no longer agrees with reality.

Spatial disorientation may lead to sensory illusions, which may cause the pilot to lose control of the aircraft. Pilots call the most common sensory illusion the "graveyard spiral." The pilot feels a sensation that his wings are maintaining level flight. But in reality, his aircraft has entered a steep turning-dive. This sensory illusion often proves fatal.

That's why flight instructors train their students to fly *only* using their cockpit instruments. "Flying by the instruments" gives you an objective way to judge your direction, altitude and speed. In the same way, Scripture supplies us with an objective moral standard by which we can compare our attitudes and actions.

If we trust our own sense of right and wrong, it will leave us morally disoriented. And that could lead to disaster. Or as the author of Proverbs puts it: "There is a way that seems right to a man, but in the end it leads to death" (Proverbs 14:12).

Disciplining Children

American parents show reluctance to practice discipline. Some parents seem trapped in denial about their kid's unruly behavior. They refuse to face the facts about their kids.

Others attempt to discipline, but fail to hold their ground. Their kids find ways to wiggle their way out of trouble. They give in to their toddler's tantrums, they crumple under their child's manipulation or their teenager manages to wear them down.

In other cases, disengagement drives permissiveness. Career and hobbies act as blinders, preventing parents from seeing the kind of trouble their kids are getting into. Or parents can't summon the energy to discipline due to exhaustion from work or chasing toddlers all day long.

Still others refuse to discipline because they can't bear seeing their children upset. They tell themselves, "She'll grow out of it" or "They're too young to understand." But they fail to see the extent to which the Fall distorts human nature.

The book of Proverbs approaches parenting holding two basic assumptions. One, love requires discipline. Proverbs 22:15 states, "Folly is bound up in the heart of a child" and it takes more than words to dislodge it.[1] Two, parents may need to introduce temporary pain in order to see lasting results. Parents can establish a pattern of living that will serve as a reference for their children in adulthood. "Train up a child in the way he should go, and even when he is old he will not depart from it" (Proverbs 22:6).

We need to take a long-term view with discipline. Just because something causes temporary discomfort or pain doesn't mean it's harmful. Clinical psychologist and Christian author Henry Cloud provides a helpful distinction between "hurt" and "harm."

We all hurt sometimes in facing hard truths, but it makes us grow...That is not harmful. Harm is when you damage someone. Facing reality is usually not a damaging experience,

---

[1] Kidner, *Proverbs*, 47.

even though it can hurt.[2]

However, it's not enough for parents to discipline their kids. Parents must discipline for the right reasons. Many parents wage war with their kids over minor issues. But when you emphasize everything, you emphasize nothing. Parents must learn to pick their battles carefully. For instance, many parents will ground their kids for bad grades or arriving five minutes after curfew. But they won't say anything when they find out their kids are falling into sexual immorality.

So where should we place our emphasis? In his excellent book *Revolutionary Parenting*, Christian sociologist George Barna sifted through more than 10,000 personal interviews of people he identified as "Spiritual Champions." Spiritual Champions describe radically committed followers of Christ. He sought "to find out what had happened during their formative years that led them to become irrepressible followers of Christ."[3] By studying these interviews, Barna uncovered the common link between Spiritual Champions. They all grew up with "Revolutionary Parents."

In a quarter century of doing research I have rarely encountered instances where 100 percent of the group being studied agreed on something. Yet, every single Revolutionary Parent we interviewed agreed that the most important focus of their children's training was the development of godly character.[4]

Barna observes, "Spiritual champions have the advantage of being raised by parents who are more concerned about the love they show fellow students than whether they outperform them."[5] He

---

[2] Henry Cloud, *Necessary Endings: The Employees, Businesses, and Relationships That All of Us Have to Give Up in Order to Move Forward* (New York: Harper Collins Publishers, 2010), 21.

[3] George Barna, *Revolutionary Parenting: Raising Your Kids to Become Spiritual Champions* (Carol Stream, IL: Tyndale House Publishers, 2007), XIX-XX.

[4] Ibid., 46.

[5] Ibid., 47.

recounts what one Revolutionary Parent said about the challenges of raising a Spiritual Champion:

> "Oh my gosh" said a mother, laughing as she recalled the behavior of her son, who was always trying to impress his folks with his grades and his sports feats. "We kept coming back to how he treated people and what he did with his money...We tried to affirm his accomplishments, but we worked at keeping those things in their proper place. He was sick of hearing me tell him that I'd rather have an honest boy than a smart one, and that God was more excited about a servant than a superstar.[6]

This emphasis on character snaps together with the priorities we see in Scripture. In 1 Timothy 3:1-6, Paul provides us with a list of qualities found in an elder or a leader in a church. The Greek word for elder literally means "older man." Therefore, you could expand its application to include qualities found in spiritually mature believers.[7] Oddly, Paul never mentions spiritual gifting in his list. All but one of the qualities refer to a person's character.

When Jesus envisioned the world's first impression of his followers, he didn't say, "They will know that you are my disciples by your *intense commitment* to follow me." He didn't say, "They will recognize you as my followers by your *extremely moral behavior*." He said, "All men will know that you are my disciples *if you love one another*" (John 13:35, emphasis mine). Paul echoed this when he declared love as the goal of his instruction (1 Timothy 1:5). He claimed that the absence of love would empty faith and self-sacrifice of their value (1 Corinthians 13).

Therefore, parents should nurture their children's ability to love. They should emphasize the relational and spiritual areas of life over every other area. The emphasis on love also suggests that parents discipline for behavior that harms relationships, such as nourishing bitterness or lashing out with their words.

---

[6] Ibid., 48.

[7] Gene Getz, *Measure of a Man*, 16-18.

Parents shouldn't downplay their role in molding their child's character. Henry Cloud highlights the importance of parents in character formation.

When you are a parent, you help create a child's future. The patterns children establish early in life (their character) they will live out later. And character is always formed in relationship. We can't overestimate your role in developing this character. As Proverbs says, "Train a child in the way he should go, and when he is old he will not turn from it" (Proverbs 22:6).[8]

However, discipline doesn't guarantee obedience. Even the best training may fail to impart wisdom. Self-will may prevent a son or daughter from listening (Proverbs 13:1). And even a good home may produce a sluggard, someone trapped in sexual immorality or a person callous enough to steal from his parents (Proverbs 10:5; 29:3; 28:24).

Parents can only do so much. I've witnessed godly parents try to cultivate a love for God in their children. But their son or daughter refused to follow God.

Luckily, the story isn't over. God continues to pursue these children through the Holy Spirit's conviction (John 16:8) and he eagerly awaits their return (Luke 15).

Reluctance to Discipline

Many people in our culture feel reluctant to discipline. We can list several reasons for this reluctance.

For some, discipline was absent from their home growing up. Either their parents let them do whatever they wanted or they never got into trouble. I've met people who couldn't even furnish one example of their parents disciplining them. Therefore, they lack a category for correction or loving discipline.

For others, discipline was present at home. But their parents disciplined them out of anger. Discipline didn't represent an act of

---

[8] Henry Cloud and John Townsend, *Boundaries with Kids: When to Say Yes, How to Say No* (Grand Rapids MI, Zondervan, 2009), 15-16.

loving correction. It served as a release valve for building frustration. At times, these outbursts took the form of verbal abuse. At other times, it turned physical or escalated into a scuffle. As a result, they've swung to the opposite extreme. They're reluctant to discipline because they associate it with abusive behavior.

Still others try to compel change through sheer love. They maintain that "if you love someone" they'll eventually change. They assure themselves, "Stick in there with them and sooner or later they'll get it." But many biblical examples contradict this view. For example, Jesus cried out:

> O Jerusalem, Jerusalem, you who kill the prophets and stone those sent to you, how often I have longed to gather your children together, as a hen gathers her chicks under her wings, but you were not willing. (Matthew 23:37)

Jesus spent large quantities of time and energy persuading people to put their faith in him, yet most refused.

A handful tell themselves, "I just love her too much to say anything." But if you love someone and see a destructive pattern in her life, it would compel you to say something. Simply showing love doesn't correct misguided thinking.

Self-absorption may also lead to softness. Some find it difficult to see issues in their friends' lives because they spend most of their time thinking about themselves. They feel blindsided when a close friend shares a struggle he has been dealing with for months.

Most of the time, you can draw a straight line connecting softness with fear. Often, we won't confront our family or friends because we don't want them to get angry with us. Our body tenses up at the mere thought of placing ourselves in an awkward conversation. So we "never get around" to bringing up issues with people. Or we postpone discussing it because "something came up."

Consequences of Permissiveness

The high price of permissiveness may end in misery, tragedy, even death. Although our culture shows contempt for people "sticking their nose into someone else's business;" on occasion, it applauds discipline. Family and friends will sometimes lure a loved one into a group intervention, to confront him/her about an addiction or mental disorder.

Scripture sees eye-to-eye with our culture on this point. Some matters are so serious, so damaging, we're practically obligated to confront our loved ones. However, Scripture disagrees with our culture about what to confront. Drug addiction and alcohol abuse may shatter someone's life. But according to the Bible, bitterness, hatred and sexual immorality may cause just as much damage (1 Corinthians 6:18; Hebrews 12:15). If we fail to speak God's truth to our loved ones on these important matters, they may continue to harm themselves and those around them.

Some people's permissiveness goes beyond holding their tongue. They actually enable their friends and family to continue their destructive ways of life. For example, a fearful wife may run interference for her husband when a close friend tries to confront him about his selfishness. She'd rather not stir up the hornet's nest when she has to live in it.

Or someone may act as a screen of protection, coming to her Christian friend's defense when someone raises an issue in her life. The person will make excuses for her, saying "She's just too fragile to face something like that right now."

In some cases, permissiveness evolves into complicity. A few parents actually finance their son's or daughter's damaging lifestyle. You see this when parents allow their hopelessly drug-addicted daughter to live with them. Or it becomes evident when parents constantly bail out their college-aged son, who maxes out his credit card and can't pay his bills. They aren't loving their son or daughter when they do these things. They're aiding in their son's or daughter's destruction. Solomon warns, "Discipline your son, do not be a willing party to his death" (Proverbs 19:18).

Failure to speak truth also leads to surface-level relating. Those who show reluctance to speak truth, spend most of their time with people making small talk. They discuss current events or talk about last night's game. But they won't bring up real issues because it feels awkward. They tell themselves, "It's none of your business." Or they convince themselves not to raise an issue with someone. "They'll probably figure it out," they tell themselves. They try to stay in their lane and keep a safe distance. Besides, they don't want to open the door to people meddling in their own affairs.

Softness often produces manipulative children. Some parents never discipline or tell their kids "no." On rare occasions, they will try to hold their ground. But their kids manage to find a way around the consequences. Manipulative children employ a variety of tactics including explosive displays of anger, crying on command and bending the truth. Over time, these tendencies harden and become second nature.

People who never encountered discipline growing up often chafe against authority. They carry around a suspicion toward authority figures. They're unwilling to take input from people. If someone confronts them, they get defensive. Or they walk around with a sense of entitlement pinned to their chest. They aren't accustomed to people telling them "no." So they manipulate or attempt to wear people down with a fusillade of requests.

Ironically, if we never discipline we're actually more prone to harshness or abuse. Frustration builds when we refuse to confront our family and close friends. And eventually it spills over in outbursts of anger and abusive behavior. I've had some of the most mild-mannered guys tearfully confess that they cussed out their wife or physically threatened their children. They refused to do anything until one day they snapped.

Overuse of Discipline

Some people take the opposite approach to discipline. They take a heavy-handed approach with people. They use discipline as their default setting. Yet, this approach may yield some unforeseen results.

Overuse of discipline impedes independent thinking. People who use discipline as their primary way to motivate often find themselves surrounded by overly compliant people. In most cases, they can raise obedient children and develop compliant Christians. Those around them enjoy the security of people telling them what to do. But they proceed with extreme caution when making their own decisions, fearing criticism or correction.[9]

Correction and rebuke may impel change, yet it may not last. Most people will comply just to get someone to stop badgering them. But they often revert to their old behavior.

Not long ago, my friend was talking about a guy in his home church who lost over a hundred pounds. My friend played a key role in helping this guy lose weight. But recently he gained it all back. My friend said, "When I asked his [new] spiritual mentor how he was going to help this guy, he told me, 'We're challenging him about gaining back his weight. We even threatened to take away opportunities for him to teach the Bible.'" But it didn't work. Months later, he was still packing on the pounds. "It occurred to me," my friend mused, "when this guy was in our group, we never admonished or rebuked him. We just painted a positive vision for him losing weight and celebrated small victories."

Also, the threat of rebuke or correction may drive people to burrow underground with their sin. For example, some parents declare war on their kids whenever they rebel. Their home turns into a battleground as they challenge their kids at every turn and they won't relent until their kids wave a white flag. But when they ratchet that much tension it often backfires. It doesn't result in their kids repenting; it turns them into trained liars. They find ways to conceal sin from their parents. Real change takes place in an atmosphere of openness, grace and patience, not criticism and correction.

God furnishes us with a variety of ways to motivate people. Therefore, we should utilize a diverse approach. Apply admonition and correction sparingly. And use generous amounts of encouragement, instruction and modeling. When Paul walked

---

[9] Bruce Powers, *Christian Leadership* (Nashville, TN: Broadman Press, 1979), 16-17.

Timothy through how to handle the distressed group in Ephesus, he could've said, "Rebuke them publicly!" But Paul's approach was far more dynamic. He tells Timothy, "Set an example for the believers in speech, in life, in love, in faith and in purity" (1 Timothy 4:12). In other words, model a life of spiritual maturity. And if Timothy must resort to rebuke, Paul tells him to "correct, rebuke and encourage—with great patience and careful instruction" (2 Timothy 4:2). Notice, Paul offers a variety of approaches alongside "rebuke," such as correction and encouragement. Paul also helps Timothy with the tone of his correction. He needs to sand down harsh edges off his rebuke, appealing to the Ephesians as he would a family member (1 Timothy 5:1-2).

Helpful Tips on Discipline

Self-righteousness repels people. It shuts people's ears to what we have to say. On the other hand, humility sets the stage for correction. It disarms people and makes them more willing to listen. Before we speak the truth in love to someone, we must first come before God and ask him to show us our own shortcomings (Gal. 6:1). This will set the tone for our conversation.

Second, sprinkle Scripture throughout your conversation. Bruce Powers points to the weakness in employing manipulation tactics. Tactics "such as getting angry, sending guilt messages, nagging and withdrawing love, usually do not motivate people to change. If they do, the change is short-lived, directed only at getting the person to lighten up on the psychological pressure."[10] Only Scripture has the power to transform people's lives.

Third, end the conversation by painting a positive vision for them gaining victory. Reaffirm your relationship. And reiterate that you're saying these things out of love. In addition to this, offer some practical steps for them to take.

---

[10] Ibid.

Speaking the truth in love can alter the course of your friend or family member's life. If you do it with a tone of grace and love, often the person you're correcting walks away feeling loved. And you can rescue them from further damage (James 5:19-20).

For Further Discussion:

1. What are some of the common fears that block us from sharing a word of correction with a friend or family member?
2. Can you add any other helpful tips for effectively disciplining?
3. Highlight some other differences between discipline and punishment.

HONING YOUR DISCERNMENT

After God anointed Solomon king, he appeared to Solomon in a dream, "Ask whatever you want and I'll give it to you." Can you imagine God giving you a blank check? "*Whatever* you want." Solomon replies, "I am like a little child who doesn't know his way around" (1 Kings 3:7, NLT). Even though Solomon was 40 years old, he possessed neither the skill nor experience to govern Israel. Solomon resembled a true freshman quarterback whose coach suddenly throws him into the big game.

Solomon does something no one sees coming. He asks God for wisdom. God looked favorably upon his request. So he gave Solomon great wisdom *and* vast wealth. Right away, people noticed something different about him. He showed remarkable wisdom.

Sometime later, two prostitutes enter Solomon's court seeking to settle a dispute. When Solomon signals for them to speak, one of the women begins accusing the other. "Master, this woman and I live in the same house. I gave birth to my son while she was there. Three days later, she too gave birth to a boy.

"In the middle of the night, she rolled over and smothered her son. When she awoke and saw what she had done, she got out of bed, took my son from my arms and laid her lifeless son by my side. When I woke up to nurse, it looked like my son had died! But when I examined him closer, it was clear..."

The other woman interrupted, "I didn't take your son!" And the two women began arguing in the king's presence.

Solomon began to speak and the women fell silent. "Bring me a sword," he told his servants. "Cut the baby in half. Give one half to each of these women and then bring in the next person." Stunned by the verdict, the servant slowly took the child from the woman's arms.

Just as the servant began to lift the sword over his head, the woman whose son was alive yelled, "Stop! Don't kill him. Give her the baby. Just don't harm him!" The other woman looked at her spitefully and said, "Neither of us will have him." She turned to the servant and said, "Obey the king's orders."

Solomon spoke to his servant, "Give the child to the woman who pled for his life. She's the mother."

Solomon's story in 1 Kings 3 depicts two aspects of discernment. First, Solomon skillfully brought truth to the surface. Obviously, one of the women standing before him was lying. Both couldn't have been the boy's mother. He was able to smoke out the one lying. Thus, one aspect of discernment refers to the ability to judge truth from falsehood and sound, biblical teaching from false teaching.[1]

The author of Hebrews refers to this type of discernment when he confronts his audience for their anemic Bible knowledge. "Solid food is for the mature, whose perceptions are trained by practice to discern both good and evil" (Hebrews 5:14, NET).

Second, Solomon showcased his grasp of human nature. He predicted the boy's real mother would stop at nothing to protect him. Discernment bears close resemblance to wisdom. It describes someone you might call "street smart." It points to the ability to read people and situations correctly. It represents a working knowledge of how people operate and the way they might react to certain situations.

In the following section, we'll elaborate on these two aspects of discernment. And then we'll look at some practical ways to hone each.

Discerning Truth from Falsehood

The New Testament writers spilled a lot of ink to help us identify false teaching. Jesus warns us of false prophets, picturing them as ferocious wolves dressed in sheep's clothing (Matthew 7:15). The

---

[1] We shouldn't confuse the skill of discernment with the gift of discernment. In 1 Corinthians 12:10, Paul refers to the supernatural ability to detect demonic activity, in a way others cannot.

Apostle John gives us ways to spot counterfeit christs (1 John 2:22-23). Paul cautioned the Ephesian elders to "keep watch" in his farewell speech. "Savage wolves" he predicted, "will come in among you and will not spare the flock" (Acts 20:29).

Make no mistake; discerning truth from falsehood isn't easy. If it were obvious, then we wouldn't see false teachers ripping away large swaths of the American church. False teachers ooze charisma and charm. They draw a following by telling people whatever their itching ears want to hear (2 Timothy 4:3). That's why Paul insists we judge people by what they say, not by how they look. "For Satan himself masquerades as an angel of light" (2 Corinthians 11:14).

We could say the same for written material. Authors spend countless hours agonizing over how they can alter our views. So we must read with a critical eye. Just because something resonates with us doesn't mean it's true. We must appraise what we read by what's contained in Scripture.

Several years ago, I conducted a thought experiment on my men's small group. I was teaching from a passage of Scripture, which discusses how to discern false teaching. But before they cracked open their Bibles, I offered a suggestion, "Why don't we do something different. Let's start by looking at an excerpt from a book I've been reading." I didn't tell them that the author sought to erode the Bible's foundation by raising questions about its accuracy.

To paraphrase the section, the author said, "What if a scientist discovered DNA evidence proving Jesus had a real biological father? Could you still love God? Could you still be a Christian? Or does the whole thing fall apart?"[2]

After we read the excerpt, I said, "So what do you guys think? Do you see anything wrong with what he's saying?" No one responded. Some put their hand over their mouth and stared into the air. Others carefully reread the excerpt with furrowed brows. A

---

[2] Rob Bell, *Velvet Elvis: Repainting the Christian Faith* (Grand Rapids: Zondervan, 2005), 26.

few seconds passed and one of the guys broke the silence. He spoke with hesitation in his voice, "I don't really see anything wrong with what he's saying." Someone else chimed in, "Yeah I'm not sure it would crush my faith." Most nodded their heads.

Then I pointed out, "Why did this author choose to raise doubts about the virgin birth? If you could prove Jesus had an earthly father, wouldn't that imply Jesus was just a man? Wouldn't it undermine his divine nature?" Instantly, one of the guys said, "Yep...that's a problem." Others added their concerns. Once they could see the implications of what the author was saying, they were able to uncover the problems of his argument.

Honing your ability to discern truth from falsehood

First, learn solid principles of biblical interpretation. When you interpret the Bible, you're attempting to locate what the author was saying to his original audience. Most of the time, you can arrive at the original meaning through a common sense reading of the text.[3] Try to draw the meaning out of the text, rather than importing a meaning into it.

Second, read Christian books critically. Try to ask yourself, "What is the author leaving out?" Run these questions through your mind:

What are the implications of what the author is saying?

Does it undermine the authority of God's written word?

Does this fit with what the Bible emphasizes?

It's not enough to teach what the Bible teaches. Balanced biblical teaching stresses what the Bible stresses. Scripture speaks to a variety of topics. And it speaks truthfully about them all. But some books of the Bible occupy greater importance compared to others. For instance, the book of Obadiah pulls back the curtain and shows

---

[3] Biblical scholars sometimes refer to this as the Grammatical-Historical Method of interpretation. You can use a number of different inductive study methods to help you arrive at the author's original intent. For further reading, see *How to Read the Bible for All Its Worth* by Gordon Fee.

us why God destroyed Edom. But it doesn't stand on the same platform with other books like Romans or Genesis.

As you sit through Bible teachings or read Christian books, ask yourself, "Does this point snap together with the biblical text he's citing? Is he pulling this passage out of its context?" Pastors and teachers aren't immune to mistakes. You should question what people say when they claim to speak for God. You should be able to look down at your Bible and see what they're saying, right there on the page. Never tell yourself, "He seems like he knows what he's talking about. I'm sure he's going in the right direction with this." That's probably what lemmings say right before walking off a cliff.

Discerning People and Situations

Discernment is a close relative to wisdom. At times, the Hebrew word for wisdom (*hokmah*) refers to a technical skill such as stonework or carpentry. At other times, biblical authors use it to describe someone skilled at living. Thus, discerning people possess a deep understanding of the way people work and how they react to certain situations.

According to the Bible, humans enter the world with a dual nature. On the one hand, God made us wonderfully complex. David declares, "I am fearfully and wonderfully made" (Psalm 139:14). God created us with incredible intellect, near limitless creativity and the capacity for love and self-sacrifice.

However, Jeremiah tells us our hearts are desperately sick. "The heart is deceitful above all things and beyond cure. Who can understand it?" (Jeremiah 17:9). As humans, we use our ingenuity and creativity to invent new ways of doing evil.

Usually, people who suffer from bad discernment hold a faulty view of human nature. An imbalanced view of our dueling natures often leads to bad discernment. Let's examine both extremes.

Seeing the Best in People

If we hold a distorted view of human sinfulness, we tend to see people in an overly positive light. In particular, those who've grown up in an environment marked by secular humanism tend to view people this way. After receiving Christ, my longtime friend recalled never hearing the Gospel at the church he attended as a kid. The revolving door of pastors never spoke about God's judgment or human fallenness. As a result, he tends to see people as naturally good.

Fifteen years ago, I visited Cambodia for the first time. The country was picking up the pieces after a violent communist regime swept through it. From 1975-1979, the Khmer Rouge butchered nearly a third of the population in an attempt to return Cambodia to an agrarian society. During my trip, a group of us visited the Killing Fields –a mass grave where the Khmer Rouge exterminated nearly 10,000 Cambodians.

Walking through the Killing Fields deepened my view of the human condition. A narrow pathway slithered through what looked like impact craters. Rain and erosion unearthed pieces of cloth, teeth and bone fragments along the path. Stations with hand painted signs depicted the horrifying ways teenage soldiers executed their victims. The tour ended at a tall pagoda faced with acrylic glass. It contained 5,000 human skulls stacked in rows all the way to the top.

On the bus ride back to the hotel, everyone sat in silence as the engine whined. When we arrived at the hotel, we filed into a small room to debrief. When everyone sat down, our guide broke the silence. "Many of you are asking yourselves, 'How could anyone do this to another human being?'" People sat up in their seats. He quickly answered his own question, "If you want to know the answer, you don't need to look any further than right here," as he pointed to his heart.

Imagine someone shoving an AK-47 into your hands and telling you to kill the blindfolded woman kneeling in front of you. They threaten to kill your family if you refuse. What would you do? Could you say with confidence you wouldn't pull the trigger? Even the most mild-mannered person will commit unspeakable acts of evil when under duress. Thus, people will commit sins that seem out of character, given the right situation.

So how can we detect if we possess a skewed view of human nature? Let me point to a few skewed lines of reasoning. Some people may think, "If I just hang in there with people, they'll eventually change." But I've seen people reach their lowest point and continue to shake their fist at God.

At other times, you'll hear people say, "She would *never* _____." Fill in the blank. "He would *never* take money from his roommates." Really? If he overdrew his bank account and collected money for bills, couldn't you envision him using some of that money? Or, you'll hear people say, "She would never lie to me." Really? Are you saying she would never lie under any circumstances? Sin provides a motive for concealing truth. Recall a time when someone exposed sin in your life. Did you feel a strong impulse to minimize your guilt, to justify your actions or to leave out relevant parts of the story? That was your fallen nature surfacing.

Still others are ready to declare someone "repentant" based on an "encouraging talk" with that person. People with faulty discernment rely too much on their impressions rather than on facts.

Experience has trained the discerning not only to hear what a person says, but also to see what he or she does. The discerning might say something similar to the undiscerning. "We had a good talk." Yet, they're careful to add, "But we'll see how he responds."

Seeing the Worst in People

Some people display bad discernment because they see the best in people, others because they see the worst in them. They rarely give people the benefit of the doubt. They naturally conclude people aren't doing what they're supposed to do.

A few years ago, my leadership team was discussing ways to nudge a woman (in our group) to transition out of her high school ministry role. She was burning the candle from both ends and you could tell she felt overwhelmed. So we were trying to lighten the heavy load she was carrying. At one of our leaders' meetings, we asked one of our women leaders to talk to her about the possibility of transitioning. A few weeks passed and we hadn't heard anything about her conversation. Frustrations surfaced as one of our leaders said to the woman who was supposed to talk to her, "You really need to have this talk with her. It's time sensitive."

She sat in silence.

He kept going, "And you should point out that she's been checked out for the last few months."

She still didn't respond.

Finally, he said, "When do you plan on having this conversation with her?"

Then, she calmly replied, "We talked about it last week and I made that point with her."

The blood drained from his face. If he had bothered to ask a few clarifying questions, this interaction would've gone better. He should've heeded the warning from Proverbs 11:12, "The one who denounces his neighbor lacks wisdom, but the one who has discernment keeps silent" (NET).

Others allow their suspicions to tint their view of people. They always suspect people are conniving to gain an unfair advantage. They routinely jump to conclusions, only to stumble upon key facts later.

If you find yourself doing this, save yourself some trouble and embarrassment. Ask questions first. Also, give people the benefit of the doubt until you gather all the facts. In the absence of information, withhold judgment.

Still others allow negativity to block them from seeing people's potential in Christ. It may lead them to dismiss someone as "a hopeless case." "They'll never change," they murmur while shaking their heads. So they ignore that person, hoping he goes away. Thankfully, God never gives up on us. He steadily works in our lives, to give us both the desire and power to do what pleases him (Philippians 2:13). Therefore, labeling someone a "waste of time" directly negates what God says about that person.

Strangely, negative people usually apply their pessimism in a selective manner. They're unduly harsh with people outside their inner circle, but they fail to see glaring problems with those closest to them. They seem blindsided when a young believer they've been mentoring abandons her walk with God. "It just came out of nowhere. I didn't see this coming," they say. Discerning people can see that their own objectivity blurs if they're too close to someone. So they make a conscious effort to fight this weakness by asking for outside advice.

Seeing people in a negative light may also lead us to judge their motives. In the absence of information, we should resist the impulse to fill in the blanks. Interpreting people's motives may lead us to dismiss relevant facts that could steer us toward the right conclusion. Some of us judge people's motives to undermine their credibility. "She's just saying that because she's bitter." What's the subtext? We shouldn't listen to her.

At other times, people rely too much on one approach for evaluating people or situations. This also leads to faulty discernment. Let's look at three imbalanced approaches.

Case Law Approach

Some people make bad judgment calls because they use what you might call a "case law approach." When they face a confusing situation, they search their mental index for similar cases. Then they decide what they will do based on past precedents. The case law approach suffers from overly formulaic thinking. It fails to see the differences between current and past cases. Often, good discernment comes from seeing these differences and resisting a wooden approach.

Now I'm not suggesting it's pointless to examine past cases. Our discernment should grow as we gain more ministry experience. But we shouldn't use it as the sole deciding factor.

Intuitive Approach

Instead of scanning through a catalogue of past precedents, some use their initial impression as a starting point. Highly intuitive people get strong impressions about a person or situation. At times, these impressions lead to a flash of insight. But in other cases, they lead to poor discernment. Once highly intuitive people grab onto an impression, it's hard for them to let go of it. They find it difficult to adjust their initial impression to fit with emerging facts.

Now the most discerning people I've met tend to be intuitive thinkers. But they check their impressions with the facts and they let the facts refine their intuition.

Black-and-White Thinking

People trapped in black and white thinking often paint in extremes. Every situation contains either a right or wrong solution. They have trouble seeing grey areas.

Black-and-white thinkers often barge into a situation armed with an overly simplistic answer. They try to apply off-the-shelf solutions without fully understanding the problem. By contrast, discerning people can spot the complexity of a situation and they see several ways to approach solving the problem.

Honing your ability to discern people and situations

Oddly, those lacking in discernment often view themselves as discerning. So how do you discern if you lack discernment? Maybe ask yourself this question: Do you find yourself making many of the mistakes mentioned above? If so, discernment may not be your strength. Admitting your weakness in this area might be the first step toward improving your discernment.

Second, make sure sin isn't clouding your perception. When Jesus warned about the dangers of materialism, he said, "If your eyes are bad, your whole body will be full of darkness" (Matthew 6:23). He explains that your vision blurs when you find yourself entangled in hypocrisy.

How can you say to your brother, 'Let me take the speck out of your eye,' when all the time there is a plank in your own eye? You hypocrite, first take the plank out of your own eye, and then you will see clearly to remove the speck from your brother's eye. (Matthew 7:4-5)

We can eliminate blind spots in our discernment when we resolve controversies between God and ourselves.

Third, ask God for discernment and wait on his answer. James says, "If you need wisdom, ask our generous God, and he will give it to you. He will not rebuke you for asking" (James 1:5, NLT). In some cases, we may need to persist in prayer before he gives us wisdom.

Fourth, seek counsel. Proverbs 11:14 says, "When there is no guidance a nation falls, but there is success in the abundance of counselors" (NET). Or look at what Proverbs 12:15 has to say: "The way of a fool seems right to him, but a wise man listens to advice." People whom I regard as discerning regularly seek counsel from wise friends.

Fifth, surround yourself with people who possess reliable discernment. God has provided a variety of gifts in the Body of Christ. In this way we can help one another and rely on each other's strengths.

Sixth, ask good questions and listen. Often we miss crucial pieces of information because we aren't listening. "Spouting off before listening to the facts is both shameful and foolish" (Proverbs 18:13, NLT). As you listen to someone recount a story, ask yourself, "What parts of the story don't add up?" Allow facts that come to the surface to shape your conclusion. Don't put too much weight on your intuition, especially if it doesn't seem to align with the facts.

Finally, keep the door open for people to give you input. Misguided self-confidence is the leading cause of bad discernment. Proverbs 17:10 says, "A rebuke makes a greater impression on a discerning person than a hundred blows on a fool" (NET). Discerning people don't resent input; they seek it.

For Further Discussion:

1. What are other ways to discern if discernment isn't your strength?
2. Often people suffering from faulty discernment view people in an overly positive light. How do you develop a more realistic view of people without falling into negativity?

SCOOPING FIRE INTO YOUR LAP

Fire possesses great potential for both good and bad. When you use it responsibly, it can be very good. It possesses life-giving power. It can keep you warm. You can use it to cook meals. It even provides enjoyment as friends sit around a campfire talking and laughing into the late night hours. But fire can also unleash havoc. A wildfire can wipe out thousands of acres of forest and consume an entire city. In the same way, sex possesses both life-giving power and great potential for harm. Or to paraphrase my friend, "Fire can be good. But fires weren't made to be in your lap. That's not what laps were made for."[1]

Many of us never received much direction on the topic of sex. We had to figure things out on our own. Most of our parents never gave us "the talk." Maybe they felt awkward about it. Maybe, they told themselves, "They'll figure it out." Or maybe they gave us the sex talk too late. Sadly, our friends, the internet and pornography got to us first. These shaped the way we viewed sex while the cement was still wet. But Solomon didn't miss a chance to warn his children about the dangers of sexual sin.

> My son, obey your father's commands, and don't neglect your mother's instruction...For their command is a lamp and their instruction a light; their corrective discipline is the way to life. It will keep you from the immoral woman, from the smooth tongue of a promiscuous woman. Don't lust for her beauty. Don't let her coy glances seduce you. For a prostitute will bring you to poverty, but sleeping with another man's wife will cost you your life. Can a man scoop a flame into his lap and not have his clothes catch on fire? So it is with the man who sleeps with another man's wife. He who embraces her will not go unpunished. (Proverbs 6:20-29, NLT)

---

[1] Scott Risley

Now Solomon only refers to sleeping with prostitutes and adultery. He doesn't mention sex before marriage. In fact, the Old Testament hardly mentions it. Perhaps it's because ancient people married during their teenage years. Therefore, the most common form of sexual sin was adultery.

When we flip ahead to the New Testament, its authors use a broader Greek term (*pornea*) to describe sexually immoral behavior. By the way, that's where we get the term *pornography*. *Pornea* covers a wide range of sexual activities. It refers to any act that falls outside of a committed marriage between a man and a woman (cf. Genesis 2:24 and Matthew 19:3-5).

Some legalistic Christians argue that if you're not performing coitus, then you're not having sex. But according to the definition of *pornea*, "doing everything but" still counts as sexual sin. Of course, modern technology has challenged traditional definitions of sexual sin. The digital age has extended the boundaries of *pornea* to include sexting, internet pornography and even virtual reality.

The World's View of Sex

Now you would expect Christians to look different from the rest of the world in this area (Ephesians 5:3). After all, the Bible plainly warns us of the dangers of veering off the path God has marked out for sexuality (1 Corinthians 6). But according to Mark Regnerus, Professor of Sociology at the University of Texas, Christians don't differ much from the rest of the world:

> Over 90 percent of American adults experience sexual intercourse before marrying. The percentage of evangelicals who do so is not much lower. In a nationally representative study of young adults, just under 80 percent of unmarried, church-going, conservative Protestants who are currently dating someone are having sex of some sort.[2]

---

[2] Mark Regnerus "The Case for Early Marriage," Christianity Today, last modified July 31, 2009, http://www.christianitytoday.com/ct/2009/august/16.22.html

He points to people marrying later as the main reason for this startling number. The Census Bureau reports that the median age of first marriages has risen by 5 years from 1970-2015. During the 70s, people were getting married in their early 20s. Now they're waiting until their late 20s. Regnerus points out, "That's five additional, long years of peak sexual interest and fertility." Again, Christians largely follow our culture's lead.

> Evangelicals tend to marry slightly earlier than other Americans, but not by much. Many of them plan to marry in their mid-20s. Yet, waiting for sex until then feels far too long to most of them. And I am suggesting that when people wait until their mid-to-late 20s to marry, it is unreasonable to expect them to refrain from sex. It's battling our Creator's reproductive designs.[3]

Sadly, many Christian parents push their kids to wait for marriage. Mimicking the culture, they insist their kids finish their education, launch their careers and attain financial independence before marriage. "Most young Americans no longer think of marriage as a formative institution," Regnerus observes, "but rather as the institution they enter once they think they are fully formed."[4] Like people in the world, many Christians view marriage as a capstone that completes their life of success. But in the meantime, they have no outlet for their pulsating sexual drive.

Christians not only mimic our culture in practice, but have also embraced its perspective on sex. Let's turn our attention to some common views our culture holds about sex.

"Sex isn't a matter of right or wrong; it's a matter of personal preference"

Suppose someone came up to you and asked, "What's the best flavor of ice cream? Let's say you answer, "Mint Chocolate Chip," which happens to be my favorite. Suppose that person said, "That's

---

[3] Ibid.

[4] Ibid.

incorrect. The right answer is Rocky Road. It's clearly the best." You would probably say he's confused. There's no right or wrong answer to this question. Your favorite color or the type of music you enjoy are matters of personal taste.

In our modern American culture, sex falls into the same category. Sex has nothing to do with right and wrong. It's a matter of personal preference or sexual orientation. Of course, people still view certain things as taboo or "wrong," such as pedophilia. But, as our culture continues to blur the lines of sexual morality, how much longer will that last?

By contrast, Scripture teaches that sexuality falls within its jurisdiction. God made us a certain way. We're free to contradict it. But each time we step outside of God's design, we're tearing the sensitive spiritual fibers of our soul. Sexual immorality not only damages us, but also the person with whom we committed immorality. We may not notice it at first, but the scarring becomes visible when we try to form a long-term committed relationship. The damage also shows up when we try to engage in sexual intimacy with our spouse. It's impossible to erase the images of past sexual experiences branded in our minds. That's one of the reasons why God tells us to avoid sexual immorality. He sees the kind of damage we can do to ourselves if we don't heed his warnings.

Sometimes you'll hear people say, "Well, the biblical view of sex is outdated. After all, people lived different lives back then. They got married much earlier than we do today."

Others would say, "I just think that the truths of the Bible should change with the times." Two responses come to mind.

First, whenever you look at passages that teach against sexual immorality, the biblical writers back up their argument with universal, timeless truths. For example, Paul warns the Corinthian believers to "flee from sexual immorality" (1 Corinthians 6:18). Then he asks them, "Do you not know that your body is a temple of the Holy Spirit, who is in you, whom you have received from God?" (1 Corinthians 6:19). In other words, since the Holy Spirit indwells believers, we shouldn't defile our bodies by engaging in sexual immorality.

Secondly, even though our view of sex has changed, God hasn't changed at all. According to the Bible, we derive our sense of morality from God's character (1 Peter 1:15-16). God's character never changes. He's the same, yesterday, today and forever. That means morality is fixed and unchanging.

"There's nothing wrong with having sex, as long as it's consensual"

Many would say it's okay to have sex outside of marriage as long as you practice safe sex. However, Scripture tells us there's no such thing as safe sex when you venture outside of God's design. According to the Bible, casual sexual encounters leave a tough residue that's hard to get rid of.

In the movie "Vanilla Sky," David Aames, a self-indulgent publishing mogul (played by Tom Cruise) establishes a "friends-with-benefits" relationship with his friend Julie (played by Cameron Diaz). When Aames falls in love with another woman, his jilted partner baits him to get into a car with her. As they are driving along, Julie explodes into a jealous rage and crashes the car hoping to kill both of them. During this scene, I remembered one line from her tirade that struck me, "Do you know that when you sleep with someone, your body makes a promise whether you do or not?"

I have seen this happen numerous times. Two people set up an arrangement where they sleep with each other, but with "no strings attached." On weekends, they text each other late at night to meet. But one of them always starts to develop feelings. When the other party calls for this person to stick to the arrangement, it creates feelings of rejection and hurt.

These arrangements never work because when you share sexual intimacy with someone, you're not just touching that person's body. You're engaging in the deepest form of intimacy you can share with another human being. God hardwired sexuality into every dimension of our personhood. Sex represents more than a physical act; it impacts the emotional and spiritual aspects of our being. That's why when we have sex with someone, we've created a bond with that person. And each time we break that connection, we tear the inner lining of our soul.

"You gotta test-drive before you buy"

After all, "you wouldn't go to a car lot and buy the first car you see." According to our culture, that's the same as marrying someone without sleeping with him or her. A number of years ago, I talked to woman who told me her mother criticized her for not sleeping with her boyfriend. Her mother said, "How would you know if you are compatible with him, unless you sleep with him? What if there are problems?" People are speechless when you tell them that you aren't sleeping with the person you're seriously dating.

Today, most couples (60%) live together before marriage. Between 1960 and 2011, the number of unmarried couples in America increased seventeen-fold, from half a million couples to 7.5 million couples. Couples who live together view it as a prelude to marriage. They would say, "If you live with someone, you get a better picture of what it looks like to marry that person." So are they right? At best, there's no evidence to suggest living with someone increases your odds of success in marriage. At worst, the data suggests it actually increases your odds of divorce.[5]

Aside from the data, the "test-drive-before-you-buy" view contains one obvious flaw. We're comparing a human being to a

---

[5] For further reading on this subject see: Reis, Harry T., and Susan Sprecher. Encyclopedia of Human Relationships. Volume 1. Thousand Oaks, CA: SAGE Publications, 2009. 229-231; W. Bradford Wilcox. "The Evolution of Divorce." National Affairs. Fall 2009. 81-94; Paul R. Amato, Alan Booth, David R. Johnson, Stacy J. Rogers, *Alone Together: How Marriage in America Is Changing* (Harvard University Press, 2009), 73-76; David Popenoe & Barbara Dafoe Whitehead. "Should We Live Together? A Comprehensive Review of Recent Research." Second Ed. The National Marriage Project. 2002. Rutgers University.

car. People aren't objects to test drive. We're spiritual beings bearing God's image.

Also, it turns sex into a selfish act. We're putting our partner on probation. It suggests that, "If they don't pleasure me the way I want, I'm free to dump them and find someone who will." Of course, we feel like we're expressing our love for this person. But to paraphrase a saying I heard as a young Christian, "Love can always wait to give, but lust cannot wait to take." According to the Bible, God gave sexuality to humans as the supreme way to express our love within a marriage.

When you push all of your chips into the middle of the table and give yourself to someone in marriage, it gives your relationship the strength it needs for success. Showing this kind of commitment sets the tone for your marriage.

It's an outlet for relieving emotional pain

When we feel lonely, hurt, stressed or angry, we're tempted to seek relief through pleasure. Some seek comfort through food. Others stare at a screen with zombie-like expressions plastered on their face. Still others use drugs and alcohol to deaden the searing emotional pain. Sex provides another avenue for relief. Christian psychologist and author Larry Crabb explains,

> Of course, no bodily sensation is quite so intense and pleasurable as sexual arousal and release. If we regard ourselves as mere bodies and therefore want more than anything else to find some way to feel good, then sex is the ticket.[6]

Or as comedian Woody Allen put it, "Sex without love is an empty experience, but, as empty experiences go, it's one of the best."

Bouncing from one sexual encounter to another gives us temporary relief. But it leaves us feeling dissatisfied. Again, Crabb explains,

---

[6] Larry Crabb, *The Marriage Builder: Creating True Oneness to Transform Your Marriage* (Grand Rapids: Zondervan, 1992), 91.

It satisfies the body but leaves the real person empty and despairing. It offers pleasure for the body without meaning for the person...Rather than relieving or resolving the personal problems that result from rejection or criticism, sexual pleasure merely camouflages the pain with physical sensations.[7]

Sexual immorality satisfies you in the moment like cheap Chinese takeout, but leaves you hungry a few hours later.

Taking it a step further, new research suggests casual sexual encounters may lead to depression and anxiety. Melina Bersamin, a research professor of Human Development at California State University Sacramento, says, "It is premature to conclude that casual sexual encounters pose no harmful psychological risks for young adults."[8] Her research challenges a common view in our culture that casual sex doesn't hurt anyone. Bersamin's research shows a strong correlation between casual sex encounters and anxiety/depression. College students who had recently engaged in casual sex reported lower levels of self-esteem, life-satisfaction, and happiness compared to those students who had not had casual sex in the past 30 days. These students also exhibited higher levels of general anxiety, social anxiety, and depression compared to college students who had not had recent casual sex. Bersamin explains,

> One study found that having sexual intercourse with someone only once or having sexual intercourse with someone known for less than 24 hours was significantly associated with feelings of sexual regret (Eshbaugh & Gute, 2008)...[These feelings] have been linked to poor psychological outcomes, such as lower life satisfaction, loss of self-worth, depression.[9]

This research perfectly lines up with what the Bible says about sexual immorality. We may seek sexual experiences to run from

---

[7] Ibid.

[8] Melina M. Bersamin (et al.). "Risky Business: Is There an Association between Casual Sex and Mental Health among Emerging Adults?" *Journal of Sex Research*, 51(1), 43–51, 2014. 8.

[9] Ibid., 7.

pain and suffering, but these experiences eventually lead to dissatisfaction and further unhappiness.

"The sexual revolution liberated us from our Judeo-Christian shackles"

The Counterculture of the '60s and '70s advocated "free sex," which sparked the sexual revolution in America. From that time forward, our culture viewed sex in a different light. According to our culture, the sexual revolution elevated sex to a higher status. Therefore, people could express their sexuality without feelings of shame or guilt.

But have we truly elevated the status of sex? Have we increased its value by wholesaling it? Today, people in our culture view the act of sex as nothing more than satisfying an urge, like going through the drive-thru to fill a late-night craving. Some describe it as relieving yourself, like going to the bathroom. We've managed to reduce sex into a bodily function. The world's view hasn't elevated the status of sex; it has demoted the status of humans.

"The Bible is way too restrictive"

People in our culture hold that the Bible has a low view of sex, but the Bible isn't prudish. After all, God created our nerve endings so we could feel pleasure. He created sex and commanded the first humans to have it. When he stumbled upon them in the garden, he didn't say, "What are you two doing? Why are you wrestling? Wait!" God isn't surprised that we possess a strong sexual drive. He built it into our architecture. But he sets boundaries for human sexuality because he wants to protect us from ourselves. Out-of-control sexual desires can cause long-term and widespread damage, just like flicking a smoldering cigarette out of your car window during a drought.

Scripture highlights the joy of sex within marriage. I don't know if you've ever read the Song of Solomon in the Old Testament. It's racy. According to some sources, Jewish boys didn't read it until they were 13 years old. Let me give you an example of why. Solomon wrote the following line from the perspective of a newly married man speaking to his wife, 'Your stature is like that of the palm, and your breasts like clusters of fruit. I said, "I will climb the palm tree; I will take hold of its fruit"' (Song of Solomon 7:7-8). Let me give you a hint. He isn't talking about gathering fruit. God wants us to enjoy sex, but within the set banks of the river.

Burning Yourself

Engaging in sexual immorality may have some unexpected consequences. We could catch a sexually transmitted disease (STD). But, that's really the least of our worries. You can treat most STDs.

Many experience the emptiness and misery of living an immoral lifestyle. As we mentioned earlier, recent studies found a high correlation between lower life satisfaction and sexual promiscuity. But these feelings are more acute when you're trying to follow God.

A lifestyle of immorality damages our ability to form a successful marriage. When you engage in sexual immorality, you're wearing down a groove that becomes hard to change later. When we move from one partner to another, we are creating and reinforcing a pattern of selfishness. Most people tell themselves, "I'm just having some fun right now. I plan on settling down some day." Well, it's not going to be as easy as they think. Nearly half (40-50%) of all marriages in America end in divorce. And if you track the sharp increase of divorce in America, it correlates to the sexual revolution of the '60-'70s. Those who remain married find it difficult to remain faithful to their spouses. One study found that the majority of men (50-60%) and half of women (45-55%) engaged in extramarital sex at least once during their relationship.[10]

Of course, no one feels the effects of divorce more than children. Researchers have conducted numerous long-term studies on children of divorce. The results are grim. Children of divorce suffer academically, they're more likely to face poverty and they're

---

[10] Joan D. Atwood and Limor Schwartz (2002), "Cyber-Sex: The New Affair Treatment Considerations," *Journal of Couple & Relationship Therapy: Innovations in Clinical and Educational Interventions*, 1 (3): 37–56.

at risk for juvenile delinquency. Some of these studies have been running for over 30 years. In adult life, children who grew up in divorced homes have higher instances of depression. They're at higher risk for suicide. They tend to earn less money than adults who grew up in intact families. You can measure the negative effects of divorce in almost every area. Of course, you can't measure the personal toll children of divorce face. Many of us watched our parents get divorced or grew up living in a broken home.

In some cases, sexual immorality leads to sexual addiction. Some people chase after the sensation they had during their first sexual encounter like a drug addict. They multiply partners to obtain that initial feeling of release. When more isn't enough, some turn to sexually deviant practices. Crabb states, "The natural appetite for erotic pleasure has become a mad tyrant, demanding fulfillment with no concern for either boundaries or consequences."[11]

In other cases, people swing to the opposite extreme and develop sexual dysfunctions. Instead of thirsting for sex, they recoil from it. They view sex as dirty and disgusting. In marriage, they believe that their spouse loves them. But they can't shake feeling used. Still others feel like having the same partner fails to offer enough excitement, putting them at greater risk for adultery.

Therefore, the world's view of sex isn't a sign of freedom and sexual liberation. It's a sign of spiritual poverty. We've taken God's original design and created a grotesque replica of it. We've turned sex into a meaningless act, reducing our partner into an object of our pleasure.

Breaking Free of Immorality

Some of you reading this might be struggling with sexual sin. You might feel hopelessly trapped in a pattern of sexual immorality. Let me suggest a few practical steps to escape its hold on you.

---

[11] Crabb, *Marriage Builder*, 89.

First, turn to God and bring your issue to him. In the Old Testament, authors used the Hebrew words "return" or "turn" to describe the attitude of repentance. Whenever Israel drifted from God, he would send prophets to call on them to turn back to him. In the New Testament, the Greek word for *repentance* refers to "a change of mind." It describes turning away from a certain outlook or lifestyle and adopting God's view. Maybe you resonated with the world's view of sex as you read through my description. If so, then turn to God and ask him to transform your mind by helping you adopt his view of sex (Romans 12:2).

Second, confess that you've fallen into sexual sin to a trusted Christian friend or your spouse. Sin enslaves us. When we get into trouble in this area, it's easy to think, "It was just one time. No one needs to know. I'll just make sure it never happens again." Keep in mind, God's enemy wants to neutralize your effectiveness for God. If you go underground with your sin, he'll whisper accusations into your ear, "So now you're going to act like you're spiritual? After what you have done? You're a faker. You can't let anyone know about this. You might as well quit." God's enemy wants to subdue you by making you feel alienated from God and other believers. If he can isolate you, it increases the chances of you falling back into sin.

If you're letting secret sin eat away at you, heed Solomon's warning, "The man who commits adultery is an utter fool, for he destroys himself. He will be wounded and disgraced. His shame will never be erased" (Proverbs 6:33-34, NLT). If you're living in sexual sin, you're destroying yourself and harming your ability to draw close to God.

Fortunately, the last thing Solomon said doesn't apply to us. God blotted our shame through Jesus' blood. Remember, Christ paid for all of our moral wrongdoing, past, present and future. He's already forgiven us for what we've done. That's what gives us the freedom to confess. No matter how people respond, we can be confident that God will never reject us. And if we belong to a loving fellowship, the people we think will judge us will probably give us grace. Confession often brings a sigh of relief. We find an end to the lying and hiding. In many cases, confessing brings feelings of joy and a new appreciation for God's mercy.

Third, don't play with fire. Paul gives the Corinthian believers this grave warning: "Flee from sexual immorality. All other sins a man commits are outside his body, but he who sins sexually sins against his own body" (1 Corinthians 6:18). Notice, he doesn't say, "Take your stand against sexual immorality." He tells them to flee! Our sexual desires possess too much power. Therefore, it's unwise to place ourselves in tempting situations.

Take preventative measures. Of course, this will vary from person to person. For those of us who struggle with pornography, that means getting accountability software for your computer and devices. For those of us who are falling into sin with our boyfriend or girlfriend, we may need to set some physical boundaries and avoid compromising situations. Also, ask a trusted Christian friend to keep you accountable by occasionally asking if you're struggling.

Fourth, resist and replace. We often turn to sin because we're trying to fill a void in our lives. Typically, we fall into sexual sin because we feel lonely or dissatisfied. But when we attempt to serve people and build deep relationships, the joy we feel will curb some of the temptation we feel.

Breaking free from the grip of sexual immorality starts the healing process. Immorality has left us with a lot of scarring. We can't stop ourselves from viewing people as sexual objects. We possess a distorted view of sex. And most of the time, we feel powerless to change. But God can heal us. He's powerful. He can redeem even the most damaged person.

Embracing God's Vision

Ultimately, we need to gain a vision for marriage if we want to break free of an immoral lifestyle. Our desire for sex won't go away. So we'll need to embrace an alternative to *pornea*. But this will require taking a counter-cultural stance.

Like most people in our culture, we might feel reluctant to get married in our 20s. A recent Gallup Poll showed that the number of married adults (18-24) in America dropped by 16% from 2006 to

2014.[12] Many of us fear either getting married because we watched our parents go through a nasty divorce or we've prioritized pursuing our career. So we've postponed marriage.

But if we ever hope to break the cycle of sexual sin in our lives, we need to set marriage as a goal. God's power can take someone who came out of a broken home and help him or her develop a lasting marriage. Getting married also makes financial sense. In marriage, couples share their expenses. They no longer have to pay rent and utilities on two places.

As you wait for God to send you a godly man or woman, commit to developing skills you'll need for a successful marriage. For example, you need to learn how to love sacrificially. You need to learn to how to forgive. You need to learn active listening. The best way to learn these skills is in the context of a spiritual community. I want to give you a saying that floats around our fellowship: "Shift your focus from *finding* the right person, to *becoming* the right person."

It's not surprising that our culture tells us just the opposite. "Experts" insist that compatibility determines our success in marriage. But should we build something as important as our marriage upon human speculation? If our world knows what it's talking about, where are the results? Are we willing to risk the success of our marriage on a coin flip? Reject the world's wisdom and embrace God's wisdom for building a successful marriage. He's the one who designed it.

For Further Discussion:

1. In our day, it's common for people to watch pornography. Why is watching pornography damaging to our spiritual health and relationships?

---

[12] "Fewer Young People Say I Do to Any Relationship," Gallup Poll, last modified June 8, 2015, http://www.gallup.com/poll/183515/fewer-young-people-say-relationship.aspx

2. What are some other steps you can take to prevent falling into sexual immorality?
3. When are you crossing the line into sexual immorality in a dating relationship?

WOMEN WANT TO BE HER; MEN WANT TO BE WITH HER

I live near a major university where it's common to meet college students who say the Bible discriminates against women. I can see why they feel this way. Religion hasn't exactly been friendly towards women. Many religions contain teaching that supports mistreatment of women.

But the Bible stands in sharp relief to other world religions. Scripture furnishes us with many examples of women who stood as spiritual giants. Two Old Testament books (Esther and Ruth) feature a woman as the main character. The New Testament writers sprinkle their letters with examples of women who possessed powerful faith. In addition to this, the Bible gives several reasons for holding a high view of women. For example, in Genesis 1:26, God says, "Let us make man in our image, in our likeness." God created both men *and* women as his image bearers. Thus, women enjoy equal status to men in the Bible.

Jesus put the final stamp of approval on gender equality at the cross. Paul thunders about the radical oneness we share in Christ. "There is neither Jew nor Greek, slave nor free, male nor female, for you are all one in Christ Jesus" (Galatians 3:28). It doesn't matter if you're white or black, rich or poor, male or female. We all enter our relationship with God the same way, by humbling ourselves and receiving a handout.

The book of Proverbs devotes an entire chapter to describing the virtues of a godly woman. It opens with, "The sayings of King Lemuel—an oracle his mother taught him" (31:1). It's hard to nail down the identity of King Lemuel. Some argue that Solomon wrote this chapter. If so, then Solomon was passing along his mother's (Bathsheba) advice about what to look for in a woman. Take a minute to read this remarkable description in the New Living Translation.

10 Who can find a virtuous and capable wife? She is more precious than rubies.

11 Her husband can trust her, and she will greatly enrich his life.

12 She brings him good, not harm, all the days of her life.

13 She finds wool and flax and busily spins it.

14 She is like a merchant's ship, bringing her food from afar.

15 She gets up before dawn to prepare breakfast for her household and plan the day's work for her servant girls.

16 She goes to inspect a field and buys it; with her earnings she plants a vineyard.

17 She is energetic and strong, a hard worker.

18 She makes sure her dealings are profitable; her lamp burns late into the night.

19 Her hands are busy spinning thread, her fingers twisting fiber.

20 She extends a helping hand to the poor and opens her arms to the needy.

21 She has no fear of winter for her household, for everyone has warm clothes.

22 She makes her own bedspreads. She dresses in fine linen and purple gowns.

23 Her husband is well known at the city gates, where he sits with the other civic leaders.

24 She makes belted linen garments and sashes to sell to the merchants.

25 She is clothed with strength and dignity, and she laughs without fear of the future.

26 When she speaks, her words are wise, and she gives instructions with kindness.

27 She carefully watches everything in her household and suffers nothing from laziness.

28 Her children stand and bless her. Her husband praises her:

29 "There are many virtuous and capable women in the world, but you surpass them all!"

30 Charm is deceptive, and beauty does not last; but a woman who fears the Lord will be greatly praised.

31 Reward her for all she has done. Let her deeds publicly declare her praise.

You can look at this passage in one of two ways.

You can view it the way King Lemuel intended –a description of what to look for in a woman. According to King Lemuel's mother, a young man should look at a woman's character when deciding if he should marry her. Yet, when I talk to Christian guys about dating, most seem to care more about how a girl looks than if she's spiritually minded. They care more about if she's "hot" than if she treats her friends and roommates well. But God sees past the outward appearance. He offers this perspective, "Like a gold ring in a pig's snout is a beautiful woman who shows no discretion" (Proverbs 11:22).

Or you can look at this passage as a standard, which spiritually minded women should set as their aim. It's difficult to strive for godly character when our culture prizes outward appearance over substance. Many young women feel pressure to live up to a certain standard of beauty. Billboards, magazine covers, makeup ads and "Photoshopped" images set the standard for beauty. Young women in our culture face a steady barrage of doctored images, which contain an "ideal" body shape. It's safe to say most young women in our culture struggle with body image issues, largely because they compare themselves to unrealistic standards of beauty.

Ten years ago, Dove® launched their "Real Beauty" campaign aimed at helping women overcome a negative self-image. As part of the campaign, they released a short video called "Dove Evolution." The one-minute video begins with a young attractive woman sitting down for a photoshoot. Then the video speeds up. Her appearance morphs. Makeup artists and hairstylists descend upon her. They shellac her face with makeup and slather product into her hair. The set flashes as photographers shoot the portrait.

Editors lift, elongate and soften the image, until it's ready to plaster onto a billboard. At the end, you see the billboard image juxtaposed with a screenshot of the model before her transformation. They differ so much that you couldn't pick her out of a line-up based on the final product.

Our world promises young women, "If you want a good life, if you want happiness, then you need to look a certain way." That's why so many young women obsess over their appearance. King Lemuel's mother advises young women to set their sights on a different target. If a woman desires great praise, she must learn the fear of the Lord (v30). In other words, she should pursue the things of God. Lemuel's mother isn't discounting beauty or slamming women who maintain their appearance. Rather, she calls attention to enduring qualities that don't fade with time. As an older woman, she's able to look at things from a different perspective, "Beauty does not last; but a woman who fears the Lord will be greatly praised" (v30, NLT). In the last chapter, I gave you this saying, "Don't focus on finding the right person; focus on becoming the right person." The following description will give you a target at which you can take aim.

Now if you scan through King Lemuel's qualities, they're also qualities any young man should strive to attain. Likewise, they're qualities young women should look for in a man. Let's look through these qualities.

Industrious

When you read Proverbs 31, this woman's diligence jumps off the page. She works tirelessly. She doesn't suffer from any effects of laziness (v27). She's the first to arrive and last to leave. Her day starts before the sun rises while others slumber in their beds (v15). And she works well into the night while others relax comfortably on their couches (v18).

She manages to keep a hundred plates spinning at the same time. She oversees a large household and runs a profitable business out of her home. Yet, nothing escapes her attention. "She carefully watches everything in her household" (v27, NLT). The boundaries of her rule extend beyond her house. She purchases properties from the profit her business generates (v16). She trains younger women in godliness during her spare time, offering them wisdom and instruction (v26).

It sometimes makes my head spin watching all that my wife does in a day. She wakes up with the kids at 5:45 and chases them all day until they go to bed at 8 PM. During her day, she carefully weaves in meeting times with one or two of the women she mentors. She manages to study the Bible with these women and counsel them about their ministry despite constant interruptions from our children. Most nights of the week, she cooks homemade dinners for our family and friends who come to our house. And several nights of the week, she hauls our two young children to meetings. On top of all this, she finds time to read spiritual books and prepare Bible teachings for her women's group. My wife numbers among many women in our fellowship who diligently serve, raising a family and volunteering dozens of hours each week to ministry.

But my wife wasn't always this diligent. She would admit to you that she has struggled with laziness in the past. And she still views it as a struggle! But she has worked hard to overcome her weakness, allowing God to transform her in this area.

Possesses Knowledge and Wisdom

Lemuel's mom portrays this godly woman as someone who gives "instructions with kindness" (v26, NLT). A more word-for-word translation of this phrase might be a "law of kindness." The word "law" (in Hebrew *torah*) contains a wide range of meaning. You could translate it "commands," but it could also refer to "instruction" or "teaching." "Kindness" comes from the Hebrew word *hesed*, which the Old Testament often uses to refer to God's "lovingkindness." This was the Old Testament equivalent to the New Testament concept of "grace." So you could read this as she gives "instruction about God's grace."

All of the dynamic Christian women I've met possess a deep knowledge of God's word. They immerse themselves in Scripture and skillfully apply it in ministry. They're convinced God's word contains great power. And they've seen the Holy Spirit animate God's word to transform lives. A trained ear can detect the Scripture and biblical principles interwoven through the advice they give. These kinds of women transmit their passion for God's word to the people around them and they remain eager to learn it. They greedily devour Christian books. You overhear them discussing new insights they've foraged from their personal Bible study. And they equip others with what they've learned.

Leadership

The godly woman in Proverbs 31 exerts leadership in every sphere of life. She manages a large staff that maintains her household and keeps her business running. She gets "up before dawn to...plan the day's work for her servant girls" (v15, NLT). Her children recognize her way of life and speak highly of her. They say, "There are many virtuous and capable women in the world, but you surpass them all!" (v28, NLT). And she exercises leadership beyond the confines of her home. She gives wise counsel and instructs people about God's gracious character.

When people in our culture envision a "good Christian woman," they picture a retiring, weak, polite woman who smiles a lot. But the Bible contains many examples of courageous, strong-willed women who led God's people. Take Deborah as an example.

Deborah served as Israel's Judge. God appointed the Judges, not only to arbitrate disputes, but also to run the country and to lead Israel into battle. Some scholars argue that Deborah wasn't a Judge. That's possible. But the book of Judges makes it clear God called Deborah to lead Israel, whether by office or by default. The book of Judges introduces Deborah in the midst of a crisis in Israel. After their Judge died, Israel turned away from God and "again did evil in the eyes of the LORD" (Judges 4:1). Meanwhile, Israel's neighboring enemies (the Canaanites) were growing in military strength. The Lord turned Israel over to Jabin (the king of Hazor) who ruthlessly oppressed them for 20 years and the Israelites cried out to God for help.

Deborah enters the scene. God gives her a prophetic message to give to Barak. She tells Barak, "The Lord wants you to assemble Israel's army and to attack Jabin. He will give victory into your hands."

Barak sends a reply, "I'll go, but only if you come with me." Barak needs Deborah to hold his hand even though God promised him victory. He needs a little more assurance.

"Very well," she replied, "But because of the way you are going about this, the honor will not be yours, for the LORD will hand Sisera [Jabin's general] over to a woman" (Judges 4:9). Remember, Barak and Deborah lived in a male dominated society. So it would've heaped further disgrace upon Barak for God to hand victory over to a woman.

So Barak marshals Israel's forces to Mount Tabor, taking the high ground. Sisera's army possessed iron chariots. As far as we know, the Israelites were unable to smelt iron at this time. They probably wore bronze armor, which iron could easily pierce. Sisera marches his soldiers and chariots through the valley leading to the base of Mount Tabor. At Deborah's word, Barak leads 10,000 troops down the slopes of Mount Tabor into battle. As the forces clash, God throws Sisera's warriors and charioteers into confusion. And the Israelites rout Jabin's army.

Meanwhile, Sisera escapes on foot to a neighboring village. Frantically, he tries to find a safe house in which to hide. He finds one of Jabin's allies (Jael) and pleads with her to hide him. She brings him into her tent and puts a blanket over him. From under the blanket, Sisera asks Jael, "Do you have some water for me to drink?" Jael didn't have any water, so she gave him the next best thing. She opened up a skin of milk and gave him a drink. There's nothing like warm milk from an animal bladder to quench your thirst. After taking a drink, Jael again covered him with the blanket.

A few hours later, Barak arrives. But he's too late. When Sisera had fallen asleep from exhaustion, Jael had grabbed a hammer and a tent peg. She crept up on Sisera and drove the tent peg through his temple, pinning him to the ground. He never even saw it coming. Thus, Jael fulfilled Deborah's prophecy. On that day, Deborah composed and sang a victory song. In it, Deborah praises Jael for the critical role she played in Israel's victory, "Most blessed among women is Jael...May she be blessed above all women who live in tents" (Judges 5:24, NLT).

The Bible contains many other examples of powerful women leaders. Queen Esther risked her life in an effort to save her people. During Paul's second missionary journey, he met a dynamic couple name Aquila and Priscilla. After they met Christ, they immediately devoted themselves to his service. Aquila and Priscilla trained Apollos, whose apostolic gifting made a huge impact on the early church. They accompanied Paul during his missionary journey and traveled to different cities strengthening believers. Sometime later, Paul begins to refer to them as "*Priscilla* and Aquila." In the ancient world, it was customary to mention the more prominent person first. Priscilla probably stood out as the more gifted of the two.

Scripture gives us a different picture of godly women. The women we've looked at are far from weak and docile. They're women filled with courage, they showed fierce determination in the face of adversity and they were outstanding in their service to God.

Possesses Godly Character

King Lemuel's mother tells him to search for a woman with godly character. She appraises the value of a godly woman as "worth far more than precious rubies" (v10). Lemuel's mom describes this woman as someone who "fears the Lord." As we said in an earlier chapter, possessing the fear of the Lord refers to holding God in reverence. It means seeking God's will as you make plans for your life (Proverbs 3:5). It also means showing enough humility to trust God with all your heart (Proverbs 3:6).

Often, we select someone we want to date based on superficial things. "They need to like good music," we say. Or, "They need to be athletic." Or we want to find someone who shares our love for horseback riding. We may regard these as the most important qualities to look for in someone we want to date or eventually marry. But honestly, these kinds of things don't play a huge factor in a successful marriage. As a married person, I can attest to the advice King Lemuel's mom gave him. Godly character and relational maturity lay the foundation for a good marriage. Immaturity and character flaws act as accelerants, fueling conflict in marriage. Birdwatching or a shared love for board games may add enjoyment to an already good marriage. But it can never serve as a substitute for relational skills and godly character. Plus, it's nice to have a hobby that you can enjoy without your spouse. Married people need some space too.

But here's the catch. We're not in the best position to judge if the person we want to marry possesses these qualities. Our vision gets blurry when we're intoxicated with love. Infatuation makes it difficult to see our girlfriend or boyfriend's weaknesses. When we're drunk with love, we tend to downplay his or her character flaws. And we're more likely to declare that he or she has seen victory with only a small amount of progress. When we hear someone complain about our boyfriend or girlfriend, it doesn't fit with what we see.

Yet, people tend to put their best foot forward when they spend time with their boyfriend or girlfriend. Like observing a tree to see the direction of the wind, we get a better picture of a person's character by seeing how he or she treats his or her friends.

When I started dating my wife, her taste in art and music drew me to her. These were on my list of "must haves" for a woman. Ten years later, we still enjoy visiting art museums and listening to the same music. But these aren't what I appreciate most about her. I'm most thankful for my wife's patience and her ability to nurture. When I have something on my mind, I tend to churn and brood. My wife helps calm me when I'm blowing things out of proportion. She complements me in ways I would've never predicted before marrying her. God used my superficial list of "must haves" to draw me toward a woman who offsets my weaknesses and enhances my strengths. This leads me to the next quality.

A Teammate in Ministry

Again, our culture's distorted view of Christian women doesn't fit with examples we see in Scripture. Far from weak and retiring, Proverbs pictures the godly woman playing a vital role in her husband's life and ministry. King Lemuel describes her husband as "well known at city gates" (v23). In ancient Israel, the civic leaders would assemble at the entrance of a city. They were responsible for both the administrative duties and the spiritual health of the city. Therefore, the godly woman's husband was an influential spiritual leader. But she doesn't just hide in the shadow of her husband's prominent role. He praises her publicly for her diligence, leadership and virtue (v29). What she brings to their relationship boosts his effectiveness for God. "Her husband can trust her, and she will greatly enrich his life. She brings him good, not harm, all the days of her life" (Proverbs 31:11-12, NLT). By contrast, "A quarrelsome wife is as annoying as constant dripping on a rainy day. Stopping her complaints is like trying to stop the wind or trying to hold something with greased hands" (Proverbs 27:15-16, NLT).

The godly woman's diligence allows her husband to devote himself to leading God's people. She provides for their family through her lucrative business. And she runs her large household like a well-oiled machine. But they don't live parallel lives. They don't just function as teammates. They hold a deep affection for each other. The godly woman's husband declares, "There are many virtuous and capable women in the world, but you surpass them all!" (Proverbs 31:29).

It's a blessing when God gives you a spouse that pushes you to live for spiritual things and elevates your ministry. Proverbs 12:4 says, "A worthy wife is a crown for her husband, but a disgraceful woman is like cancer in his bones" (NLT). In our fellowship, we see living examples of this. Many of our top leaders consist of couples who mightily serve God together. For example, we see couples where the husband exhibits a powerful ability to speak for God while his wife displays incredible leadership instincts. Or we see a woman express a gift for evangelism while her husband shows a unique ability to mine insights from God's word. When you see a dynamic Christian couple, the sum proves greater than its parts.

Prioritizes Godly Values

King Lemuel tells us that this spiritual woman possesses a heart for the poor. She doesn't spend the profit from her business on frivolous things. She uses it to meet the needs of the poor. What a person does with her wallet tells you a lot about what she values. Jesus said, "Wherever your treasure is, there the desires of your heart will also be" (Matthew 6:21, NLT).

Also, the godly woman of Proverbs puts her family first. As we just mentioned, she loves her husband and works to maintain a good marriage. But she also devotes herself to her children. She anticipates their needs and diligently meets them (v15). Her way of life earns respect from her children. As a result, her children speak highly of her and praise her for her godliness (v28).

Final Plea

A mature Christian once told me, "Aside from receiving Christ, who you marry is the most important decision you can make." Nearly two decades of working with college-aged people has more than verified this statement. I've met dozens of men and women that I felt confident would make a huge impact for God. But many of them never reached their potential because they married someone who lacked a spiritual mindset. Most refused to let God transform their values and desires and let the world's values drive their selection for marriage (Romans 12:2). Some let their hormones decide for them who they should marry. Or they settled because they felt desperate to marry someone.

Often people say, "I'm sure they'll change" or "I can help them move forward." I've met lots of people who pressed on toward marriage based on this reasoning. At first, they tried dragging their spouses along. But most of the time, these efforts ended in resentment.

Others point to one success story, involving someone who married a person who wasn't that spiritually minded. "Look," they say, "he turned out to be good." But for every success case, I've seen ten that ended in disaster. God has a great spiritual future in store for you. Don't gamble it on bad odds. My friend put it best. When it comes to finding someone to marry, "Run as fast as you can toward God and look to your right and to your left to see who's running beside you."

For Further Discussion:

1. Why do you think it's so hard to see someone's shortcomings while dating?
2. Why do we gravitate toward superficial qualities when selecting someone to date?

CONCLUSION

Although our upbringing forms and shapes our character, it doesn't determine our behavior. Some of us came from homes filled with abuse, addiction or dysfunction. Many of us grew up in broken homes. All of us grew up in homes that were far from perfect. As a result, we've developed insecurities, patterns of behavior and relational tendencies that create problems for us.

At times, these deficiencies produce feelings of despair. Hopeless thoughts enter our minds. "You'll never change." "What's the point in trying?" "You should give up since you're never going to change." Yet, these defeatist thoughts directly negate what Scripture says about us. God declares that we're no longer "slaves to sin" (Romans 6:6). God freed us from the bondage of sin through Jesus' death on the cross.

In addition to this, God pledges to transform our character. "Being confident of this, that he who began a good work in you will carry it on to completion until the day of Christ Jesus" (Philippians 1:6). God tirelessly works to change us and he won't rest until he's completed his work in us. Yet, this change doesn't take place automatically. God requires our cooperation in the process. He calls on us to "live by the Spirit" and to "keep in step" with the Holy Spirit's prompting (Galatians 5:25).

At other times, we seek change through self-effort. We make solemn vows to quit drinking too much or to make decisive steps toward winning our battle with pornography. We berate ourselves each time we lose our temper on our spouse. Or we cut all of our credit cards after a spending spree. However, we quickly revert back to our old behavior. Why are we unable to change? According to God, our attempts to change will be in vain unless we draw upon his power.

Scripture tells us our character transformation follows the same pattern as our initial salvation. For example, the Apostle Paul criticizes the Galatian believers for their faulty method of spiritual growth.

> Did you receive the Spirit by observing the law, or by believing what you heard? Are you so foolish? After beginning with the Spirit, are you now trying to attain your goal by human effort? (Galatians 3:2-3)

We must exercise faith in God's grace to heal us of our destructive patterns and relational problems.

Of course, all of these presuppose a relationship with God. Without the Holy Spirit's transforming power, you're helpless to change. Some of you simply assume that you're a Christian. But, you don't become a child of God by growing up in a Christian home or by regular attendance at church. John the Apostle clearly states, "To all who received him, to those who believed in his name, he gave the right to become children of God" (John 1:12). You must receive God's forgiveness by asking for Jesus' death to settle your moral debt. The moment you do this, God promises two things. One, he guarantees your future inheritance in heaven. Two, he pledges to transform your life. If you can't remember a time when you invited Christ into your life, I urge you to turn to God and make sure you're one of his children.